LEAN AND GREEN COOKBOOK 2022

Eat Your Way To Rapid Weight Loss with 1500 Days of Healthy, Tasty and Super-Affordable Recipes!
Including Fueling Hacks and Foolproof Instructions for each meal!

Katherine Williams

Table of Contents

INTRODUCTION

There are so many reasons why human beings gain weight. Before the need to lose weight arises, there must have been a weight gain already.

Weight gain can come from several causes like poor sleep, sedentary activities, excessive consumption of processed or sugary foods, and lack of exercise. It is also easy for women, to have difficulties in losing the weight gained during pregnancy or lactation.

It can be very difficult to stick to a diet plan in the quest for losing weight, due to a very busy schedule. or because it is difficult to prepare two dinners: one for you (on a diet), and the other for your family members. Luckily, Lean and Green Diet has made it a bit simple to lose weight for both males and females.

There are so many diets that claim to have long-term benefits to people. It is therefore important that you constantly do due diligence on what diet works and what diet offers short-term results.

The Lean and Green Diet is one of the hottest trends of the many diet regimens that are available in the market, and it is designed for people who want to achieve long-term weight loss. Moreover, this diet is also celebrated as one of the best diets in the United States.

Therefore, if you want to adopt this particular diet to enjoy its benefits, then this book will serve as your guide on what you need to know about it, from the basic principles to a ton of recipes you can choose from!

The recipes contained in this book have been written focusing on people that are trying to get or stay fit while struggling with a busy schedule. This book will allow you to prepare quick and easy meals that can also be enjoyed by the whole family.

Therefore, you do not need to rack your brain about what to cook for dinner…

I sincerely hope you will enjoy this book and you can get the most out of it!

WHAT IS THE LEAN AND GREEN DIET?

Lean and Green Diet Basics

Lean and Green Diet is a weight reduction or maintenance strategy, based on portion-controlled meals and snacks, that recommends eating a combination of bought, packaged food known as "fuelings", and high protein low carb meals you have to cook by yourself known as "lean and green meals".

You can choose from three different programs (depending on your initial situation, and how fast you want to lose weight):

- Optimal Weight 5 & 1 Method: 5 Fuelings + 1 Lean and Green meal
- Optimal Weight 4 & 2 & 1 Method: 4 Fuelings + 2 Lean and Green meals + 1 Snack
- Optimal Health 3 & 3 Program (the one more oriented toward maintaining weight): 3 Fuelings + 3 Lean and Green meals

Each plan follows the government's guideline that 10-35 % of the total calories come from protein.

The main peculiarity of the L&G diet is for sure the use of prepackaged foods called "Fuelings", designed to make you feel full, and give the sustainment you need in between the Lean and Green meals.

Fuelings are made up of over 60 items and include cereal, bars, cookies, shakes, and a few savory choices like mashed potatoes and soup. They are specifically low carbs but are high in probiotic bacteria (to boost your gut health) and Protein (whey and soy proteins)

Looking at the listed foods, you might think they are quite high in carbs, which is understandable, but the fuelings are composed in such a way that they are lower in sugar and carbs than the traditional versions of similar foods. The company does this by using small portion sizes and sugar substitutes.

This diet is perfect for people who do not only want to lose weight but also for people who want a transition from their old unhealthy habits to healthier ones. Thus, this is perfect for people who suffer from gout and diabetes, as well as people who are in their senior years.

Because it is a commercial diet, it has been subjected to different studies involving its efficacy. Studies have noted that people can lose weight in as little as 8 weeks, therefore this is one of the most efficient diet regimens there is that people can adapt and eventually embrace as part of their lifestyles.

What to Eat

Depending on the type of diet plan that you choose, you have to eat several lean and green meals that are comprised mainly of lean proteins and non-starchy vegetables.

Fuelings

The Lean and Green Diet is famous for its fuelings that involve pre-packaged foods. There are more than 60 soups, shakes, bars, and other fueling products that you can consume as your meal replacements.

Lean Meats

There are three categories of lean meats identified by Lean and Green Diet including (1) lean, (2) leaner, and (3) leanest. Lean meats include salmon, pork chops, and lamb while leaner meats include chicken breasts and swordfish. Leanest meats include egg whites, shrimp, and cod.

Green and Non-starchy Vegetables

Non-starchy vegetables are further identified into (1) lower carb, (2) moderate carb, and (3) higher carb. Lower carbs include all types of salad greens and green leafy vegetables. Moderate carb vegetables include summer squash and cauliflower. Lastly, high-carb vegetables include peppers and broccoli.

Healthy Fats

No dietary regimen will be complete without a controlled dose of healthy fats. These include healthy fats such as olive oil, walnut oil, flaxseed, and avocado. It is important to consume two servings of healthy fats.

Others

Once dieters can achieve their weight loss goals through meal replacements, they can start consuming other foods to maintain their ideal weight. These include low-fat dairy, fresh fruits, and whole grains.

What Not to Eat

Indulgent Desserts

This diet regimen discourages the consumption of indulgent desserts such as cakes, ice cream, cookies, and all kinds of pastries. While eating these foods is discouraged during the first few weeks of following the diet, moderate consumption of sweet treats such as fresh fruits and yogurts can be integrated into later phases of the program.

Sugary Beverages

Similar to indulgent desserts, sugary beverages are also discouraged among those who follow the Lean and Green Diet. These include soda, fruit juices, and energy drinks.

Unhealthy Fats

Fats such as butter, solid shortening, or commercial salad dressings are calorie dense and are full of unhealthy preservatives and salt, which can slow down a lot your weight loss dream.

Alcohol

Alcohol consumption is highly discouraged in Lean and Green Diet.

What are the benefits of the Lean and Green Diet?

The Lean and Green Diet is excellent for those who need a structured food plan that is easy to follow. Since it's pretty mindless to follow the diet once you have your routine down, it's great for people who are either busy or just don't like cooking.

Better for Portion Control

Perhaps one of the most challenging facets of dieting is portion control. Many people find it difficult to control the amount of food while dieting, but the Lean and Green Diet is really strict when it comes to its fueling phase as it strictly implements portion control, thanks to its pre-packaged fueling foods.

Easy To Follow

Since the diet on the 5&1 plan, depends primarily on pre-packaged foods, you are only accountable for preparing one meal a day. What is more, to make things easy to execute, each schedule arrives with food journals and sample food choices. Also, the lean and green recipes suggested by the coaches and the food journals are easy to prepare. Finally, people not interested in preparing L&G meals can purchase prepared meals named "Flavors of Home."

The prepacked Fuelings are shipped straight to your house, a degree of comfort that is not offered by many other diets. While for "Lean and Green" dishes, you would need to look for your

products, the home delivery alternative for the "Fuelings" saves time and effort. They're quick to cook and make great grab-and-go dishes once the package arrives. Also, meals are easy to compose and there is no macro or calories counting.

May Improve Blood Pressure

Via weight loss and decreased sodium intake, Lean and Green Diet may help improve blood pressure. Although the Lean and Green Diet has not been extensively studied, a 40-week report on a similar regimen in 90 individuals with extra weight or obesity showed a substantial decrease in blood pressure. Also, all the Lean and Green Diet meal plans are planned to have less than 2,300 milligrams of sodium a day, but it is up to you to use low sodium Lean and Green meal alternatives.

It Offers Continuous Support

For each weight-reduction plan, social support is a critical component of progress. The coaching service and community calls from Lean and Green Diet include built-in motivation and customer assistance.

Achieves Fast Weight Loss

To sustain their weight, most stable individuals consume about 1600 to 3000 calories a day. For certain individuals, reducing the amount to as little as 800 calories effectively ensures weight reduction. The 5 & 1 strategy is meant for accelerated weight loss, giving short-term results that positively affect your morale during your weight loss journey.

Structured Eating Plan to Remove Guesswork

Some people learn that the most daunting aspect of healthy eating is the emotional work needed to find out what to consume every day or even every dinner. Lean and Green Diet removes the burden of meal preparation and "Decision Fatigue" by delivering "Fuelings" and "Lean and Green" menu suggestions to users for clear-cut accepted foods.

Builds a Healthy Relationship with Food

The problem that makes most people revert to their old eating habits is that they do not have a good relationship with food. However, the solid and supportive community helps developing healthy eating habits.

Recommended Exercise / Water intake

Lean and Green Diet also presents trainers with directions to help you develop their "Habits of Health" company. Also, the strategy advises performing approximately 30 minutes of exercise with mild intensity every day and consuming more than 64 oz. of water daily.

Why Lean and Green Diet is so special?

Getting started is really easy and involves only registering and paying electronically to get your first package delivered to you.

Thanks to the dynamic approach, US World Report rated # 2 on their Best Quick Weight-Loss Diets ranking. Apart from being at the top of the Best Diets chart, some amazing help and ease are given to customers to make their weight loss journey smoother.

1. It is easy to pick a plan and order and automated fulfillment is possible.
2. Food preparation is easy: The most complicated directions for pre-packed meals include the inclusion of water and microwaving. It should be possible for even untrained cooks to easily tackle the lean and green dinner.
3. Mentors seek to help you develop healthier practices, allowing you access to weekly and monthly calls to give support, group activities, and the wellness support network, which comprises experts such as licensed dietitians.
4. Meals have a strong "fullness index," which indicates that the high quality of protein and fiber can leave you feeling satiated for longer.

Cons of the Lean and Green Diet Plan

Lean and Green Diet plan still has some possible downsides, particularly if you are concerned about the expense, flexibility, and choice. This book, however, is made to reduce the downsides of Lean and Green Diet regardless.

High Monthly Cost

The price may be a barrier to targeted clients. For approximately three weeks of diet foods, the 5 & 1 option varies in price from $350 to $425. When you weigh the expense of the initiative, don't neglect to take into consideration the ingredients that you may need to get to cook your "lean and green" recipes.

Includes Processed Food

While the prepacked "Fuelings" are designed with compatible ingredients, they are also clearly processed items, which for certain consumers can be a turn-off.

Calorie Restriction Effects

While the Lean and Green Diet plan stresses regularly eating during the day, only 110 calories are produced by each "Fueling". "Lean and green" recipes are limited in calories as well. Overall you can find that the diet leaves you unsatisfied and you can still feel drained and irritable more quickly.

Isolation and Boredom at Mealtimes

The social implications of cooking and consuming food will conflict with dependency on meal replacements. At home during dinnertime or while eating out with mates, users can find it uncomfortable or frustrating to get a shake.

Food Reactions

Lean and Green Diet is a high-protein diet with a protein filling up to more than a third of the daily calories. The refined, powdered form, however, may contribute to some unpleasant implications. You can feel your stomach being distended and have other unpleasant gastrointestinal repercussions. The 'blends' of powders and proteins contain certain undesirable additives that may interfere with a medicine you might be taking.

What Is the Perfect Target of People?

The simplicity of meal replacement programs that take the guessing out of weight management has long attracted customers. That's why the successful meal-replacement program in Lean and Green Diet is suggested for individuals who are too busy to prepare all three meals daily. It also reduces the hassle of shopping for every item by offering a range of food options in fueling and supplying them to doorsteps.

Lean and Green Diet is essentially intended to shed more than 15lbs of weight for healthier adults. However, they still provide programs that can be customized to fit with those with specific fitness or lifestyle conditions. There are suggestions for adults over 65 years and inactive, individuals who are quite active, people who have little weight to lose, persons who choose to add more carbs into their diet, pregnant moms, and plans for people with gout and other conditions.

LEAN AND GREEN DIET PROTOCOLS

5&1 Optimal Weight

Consuming 6 small meals a day is the 1st Healthy Habit you will absorb. On the 5&1 Optimal Weight Plan, the body goes in a gentle but well-organized fat-burning state at the same time, maintaining and retaining lean muscle mass. You can choose from more than sixty convenient, scientifically designed, and nutritionally interchangeable fuelings. Each fueling has an approximately similar nutritional profile curated by our team of skilled food scientists and refined by our registered and expert dietitians and nutrition team.

In addition to consuming 5 fuelings per day, you will learn an alternative healthy habit, which is to know how to prepare "Lean & Green" food that is perfect for you and your loved ones. You will start to absorb what optimal nutrition appears to be and soon enough, healthy eating will be considered as second nature.

4&2&1 Optimal Weight

Designed for people who need a little bit more calories throughout the day or just want to take it more easily. A lean and green meal and a snack are added in substitution to a fueling.

3&3 Optimal Health

This diet is intended for upkeep. It incorporates three fueling and three adjusted Lean and Green dinners every day.

Once you have achieved your healthy weight, it is imperative to sustain the good habits you have learned, which includes fueling your body once every two to three hours. To aid in sustaining your healthy weight, the 3&3 Optimal Health Plan stresses the importance of nutritionally well-adjusted small meals, consumed once every two to three hours, while incorporating additional food choices in their right servings.

Which Lean and Green Diet plan is good for me?

As there are so many diet plans, it is important to get in touch with a certified coach to learn about the many options that you have. It is crucial that you do not second-guess the diet plan that you are going to follow as each diet plan is designed to fit a particular profile.

GETTING STARTED WITH LEAN AND GREEN DIET

How to Start the Lean and Green Diet?

The Lean and Green Diet has two unique phases: Initial and Maintenance Phases. Upon enrollment, you will be assigned to a diet coach that will help you undertake all the necessary things to be a successful dieter.

The initial phase is when people are encouraged to limit their calorie intake from 800 to 1,000 calories until the dieter loses 12 pounds, which usually takes 12 weeks.

The maintenance phase, on the other hand, is implemented once you have already lost 12 pounds from your initial weight. During this phase, you can increase your calorie intake to 1,550 daily. This phase can last for 6 weeks. Moreover, you are also allowed to incorporate other foods such as whole grains, fruits, and low-fat dairy into your diet.

How to Follow the Lean and Green Diet?

The success of dieters largely depends on how they approach a particular diet regimen. Thus, if you want to become successful, below are the tips that you should do while following the Lean and Green Diet.

- Opt for healthy cooking methods: baking, grilling, poaching, and broiling. Avoid frying your foods as cooking oil increases the calorie content of your food.
- Portion sizes of your food should follow the recommendations. This means that the portion sizes refer to the cooked weight and not the raw weight of the ingredients that you are using.
- Opt for foods that are rich in Omega-3 fatty acids such as tuna, salmon, mackerel, trout, herring, and many other cold-water fishes.
- Choose meatless alternatives such as tofu and tempeh. They are rich in proteins but not too much on calories.
- Following the program at all costs even if you are dining out. This means that you have to consume healthy meals when you eat out and make sure that you stay away from alcohol.
- To follow the diet first off, you must start with a conversation with the Lean and Green Diet coach to determine which plan is best suited for your goal. It could be weight loss or weight maintenance, and make yourself familiar with the Plan.

How to build your own Lean and Green Meal

A lean and green meal is made of 5 to 7 oz. of a (cooked) lean protein of your choice. The more the protein is "lean" the more ounces you are allowed to eat.

In addition to that, you have to incorporate a number of healthy fats, depending on how much lean is your protein.

Lastly, you have to add vegetables. Depending on their carbohydrate content, vegetables are classified in High, Medium, or Low Carb. The lower the carbohydrate, the higher the quantity allowed to eat.

It may sound complicated but if you follow the tables below you will find that it is easier than expected. I hope you find them useful and that they will allow you to create a thousand healthy and delicious recipes!

PROTEINS FOR EACH LEAN AND GREEN MEAL

TYPE	EXAMPLE	QUANTITY	ALLOWED HEALTHY FAT
LEAN	SALMON	5oz	0 servings
	TUNA		
	FARMED CATFISH		
	HERRING		
	MACKEREL		
	LEAN BEEF		
	LAMB		
	PORK FILLET		
	CHICKEN TIGHS		
	TURKEY TIGHS		
	TOFU	15oz	
	EGGS	3	
	RICOTTA PART-SKIM CHEESE	8oz	
	TEMPEH	5oz	
	PART-SKIM CHEESE	4oz	
LEANER	SWORDFISH	6oz	1 serving
	HALIBUT		
	TROUT		
	CHICKEN BREAST (NO SKIN - 94% LEAN)		
	TURKEY BREAST (NO SKIN - 94% LEAN)		
	EGGS	2	
	EGG WHITES	4	
	2% COTTAGE CHEESE	12oz or 1 cup	
	LOW FAT GREEK YOGURT	12oz	
LEANEST	COD	7oz	2 servings
	HADDOCK		
	FLOUNDER		
	ORANGE ROUGHY		
	TILAPIA		
	GROUPER		
	HADDOCK		
	MAHI MAHI		
	WILD CATFISH		
	TUNA (CANNED IN WATER)		
	SCALLOPS		
	CRAB		
	LOBSTER		

SHRIMP		
GAME MEAT		
GROUND TURKEY BREAST		
EGG WHITES	14 or 2 cups	
SEITAN	5oz	
1% COTTAGE CHEESE	2oz or 1 ½ cups	
NO FAT GREEK YOGURT	12oz	

HEALTHY FATS – 1 SERVING

EXAMPLE	QUANTITY
OIL (EXTRA-VIRGIN OLIVE OIL WOULD BE RECOMMENDED)	1 tbsp.
REGULAR, LOW-CARBOHYDRATE SALAD DRESSING	
REDUCED-FAT, LOW-CARBOHYDRATE SALAD DRESSING	2 tbsp.
BLACK OR GREEN OLIVES	5-10
AVOCADO	1 ½
NUTS (ALMONDS, PEANUTS OR PISTACHIOS)	⅓ oz.
SEEDS (SESAME, CHIA, FLAX OR PUMPKIN SEEDS)	1 tbsp.
BUTTER, MARGARINE, MAYONNAISE	½ tbsp.

GREENS FOR EACH LEAN AND GREEN MEAL

TYPE	EXAMPLE	QUANTITY
HIGH CARB	RED CABBAGE	
	SQUASH	
	COLLARD	
	CHAYOTE SQUASH (COOKED)	
	GREEN or WAX BEANS	
	BROCCOLI	
	KABOCHA SQUASH	1 ½ cup
	LEEKS (COOKED)	
	KOHLRABI	
	OKRA	
	PEPPERS	
	SCALLIONS	
	SUMMER SQUASH	
	TURNIPS	
	TOMATOES	
	CORES	
	JICAMA	
	SWISS CHARD	
	CABBAGE	
	EGGPLANT	

MODERATE CARB	CAULIFLOWER	1 ½ cup
	FENNEL BULB	
	ASPARAGUS	
	MUSHROOMS	
	KALE	
	PORTABELLA	
	ZUCCHINI	
	SPINACH (COOKED)	
LOW CARB	ENDIVE	3 cup
	GREEN LEAF LETTUCE	
	BUTTERHEAD	
	ROMAINE	
	ICEBERG	
	COLLARD (FRESH/RAW)	
	SPINACH (FRESH/RAW)	
	MUSTARD GREENS	
	WATERCRESS	
	BOK CHOY (RAW)	
	SPRING MIX	
	CUCUMBERS	1 ½ cup
	RADISHES	
	WHITE MUSHROOMS	
	SPROUTS	
	TURNIP GREENS	
	CELERY	
	ARUGULA	
	ESCAROLE	
	SWISS CHARD (RAW)	
	JALAPENO (RAW)	
	BOK CHOY (COOKED)	
	NOPALES	

Condiment

Condiments can add more flavor to each meal or fueling you consume and, ultimately, can make the whole process more enjoyable. It is fundamental that you develop a healthy awareness of them so they can become your allies to achieve a long-term transformation. Always remember that condiments add up to your carbohydrates intake and to carefully read the labels so you can correctly dose them. The golden rule is that you can consume three servings of condiments per day in the 5&1 plan. Each serving must provide no more than 1 gram of carbohydrate per serving. Here's a table to help you in your journey!

CONDIMENT – 1 SERVING	
EXAMPLE	**QUANTITY**
DRIED HERBS/SPICES	½ tbsp.
CATSUP	
BBQ SAUCE, COCKTAIL SAUCE, WORCESTERSHIRE SAUCE	
SALT	¼ tbsp.
MINCED ONION	1 tbsp.
YELLOW MUSTARD	
SOY SAUCE	
FAT-FREE MILK/SOYMILK	
LEMON OR LIME JUICE	2 tbsp.
SUGAR-FREE FLAVORED SYRUP	
ZERO CALORIE SWEETENER	1 packet
UNSWEETENED ALMOND OR CASHEW MILK	1 cup

Snacks

The allowed snacks on the Lean and Green Diet are:

- 3 celery stalks.
- 1 fruit-flavored sugar-free Popsicle®
- ½ cup serving sugar-free gelatin, such as Jell-O®
- Up to 3 pieces of sugar-free gum or mints.
- 2 dill pickles spears.
- ½ oz of nuts: almonds (10 whole), walnuts (7 halves), or pistachios (20 kernels)

Tips for Dining Out

One of the main downsides of following a dietary regimen is that you have to give up a little of your social life.

It is difficult to enjoy a happy hour or a dinner out with your girlfriends if you follow a strict protocol and this limitation can sometimes be the reason why many people give up diet in the first place.

Luckily, you can still enjoy a dinner out with your friends at your favorite restaurant. You have only to choose the right foods from the menu or gently ask the waiter for a custom dish.

In addition, we would like to recommend the following when dining out:

- No alcohol: Alcoholic beverages are mainly empty calories. Moreover, they promote dehydration and fog your mind, causing a potential fall into not allowed foods
- Carefully research the menu before you go to the restaurant (by searching on the internet), find the right food for you, and stick to them (no dessert allowed!)
- Choose the right people: be sure to go out with people who support you and your transformational journey
- Eat mindfully: not only you will enjoy your food more but you will also increase your satiation level
- Be engaged in the conversation: you went out to stay with your friends and enjoy their company in the first place. Never forget it!
- Don't go hungry: drink plenty of water before going and try to move the fuelings closer to dinner time so you will not be so hungry
- Practice portion control: stick to the right quantity of foods for your needs.

Tips to deal with Cravings

Changing habits is never an easy task, and you may find yourself wandering near the fridge during the first days of your journey.

The good news is you are not alone: here are some tips to stay on track:

- Brush your teeth and use mouthwash
- Distract yourself with intense mental activity such as a puzzle
- Exercise or go for a walk outside
- Avoid the situations that trigger your cravings
- Drink more water

FAQ

Why Should I Try?

In any case, before you choose to pursue any program, ask yourself how you think you'll feel following the arrangement—genuinely, inwardly, and socially (regardless of whether you are shedding pounds or not). Eventually, reasonable weight reduction requires a long haul way of life changes.

Can Lean and Green Diet Help to Achieve Weight Loss?

Studies of people that have taken this diet plan show that it can be very effective in achieving weight loss than traditional calorie-restricted diets. A 16-week study conducted on 198 people who are obese or have excess weight shows that those who took the 5&1 Plan were able to lower their weight significantly as well as their waist circumference and their fat levels.

Specifically, the result shows that those that engage in the 5&1 plan were able to shed over 5.7% of their weight, and 28.1% of them were able to lose 10% of their weight. Hence, this diet plan can guarantee a 5-10% weight loss with a lower risk of type 2 diabetes and heart disease.

The record has it that those on the 5&1 diet plan and who took part in up to 75% of their coaching sessions can shed twice the weight than those that participate in fewer coaching sessions. Hence, this shows that if you take the diet plan, the coaching session is crucial as it is one of the determinants for your successful weight loss.

What are the Impacts of Calorie Restriction?

Although Lean and Green Diet's eating routine arrangement stresses eating now and again for the day, every one of its "Fuelings" just gives 110 calories. "Lean and Green" foods are additionally low in calories.

At the point when you're eating fewer calories, all in all, you may discover the arrangement leaves you ravenous and unsatisfied. You may likewise feel all the more effectively exhausted and even crabby.

Which Lean and Green Diet plan is good for me?

As there are so many diet plans offered, it is important to get in touch with a certified coach to learn about the many options that you have. You mustn't second guess the diet plan that you are going to follow as each diet plan is designed to fit a particular profile. For instance, if you are a very active person, you can take on the 5&1 plan but then, the coach will also look at other factors such as your age and health risks so that you can be matched with the right Lean and Green Diet Plan.

Can I skip the fuelings?

No. You must stick with fuelings if you want to successfully follow the Lean and Green Diet. Fuelings are designed to provide the body with balanced amounts of macronutrients that can promote an efficient fat-burning state to help people lose fat without losing energy. The problem with skipping the fueling is that you may miss out on important nutrients that might lead to fatigue while following this diet. The body feels fatigued because it cannot compensate for the lack of nutrients while being calorie deficient.

Can I rearrange my fuelings?

Yes. If you are a busy person with a dynamic schedule, then you can rearrange the timing on when you will take your fueling meals. The Lean and Green Diet is not strict about rearranging meals as long as you consume your meals within 24 hours. This versatility on your eating schedule makes it perfect for people who also have unusual schedules including those who work at night or beyond regular working hours. So, how do you time your fuelings? Just make sure that you eat your meals every two or three hours throughout the time that you are awake. Your first meal should be taken an hour after waking up to ensure optimal blood sugar levels. This is also great for hunger control.

How does it compare to other diets?

The Diet can be more viable for fast weight reduction than different plans basically because of what a limited number of calories its "Fuelings" and "Lean and Green" meals give.

U.S. News and World Report positioned Lean and Green Diet as the second-best eating routine for quick weight reduction (attached with Atkins, keto, and Weight Watchers).

The 2019 U.S. News and World Report Best Diets positioned the Lean and Green Diet 31st in Best Diets Overall and gave it a general score of 2.7/5.

Lean and Green Diet requires less "Mental Acrobatic" than contenders like Weight Watchers, (for which you need to gain proficiency with an arrangement of focuses) or Keto (for which you should intently follow and evaluate macronutrients).

The exceptionally handled nature of most nourishments you'll eat on the Lean and Green Diet can be a drawback contrasted with the variety of new, entire nourishments you can eat on increasingly independently directed plans, for example, Atkins.

Which Plan Is Best for My Level Of Fitness?

Exercise can lead to lifelong transformation. This is the reason why a specific Lean and Green Diet plan is designed for people who have different activity levels. Active adults who engage in 45 minutes of light to moderate exercise can benefit from the 5&1 Plan. Always talk with your coach about which plan is great for your age and activity level.

Tips for success

Week 1: Habits of Clean Eating and Hydration

(Health microhabit1: Consume one additional glass of water per day).

Begin the Program for Optimum Weight 5 & 1 and consume 6 tiny meals a day and consume one more glass of water a day than you do at the present day. If in the afternoon, with a snack or in the morning, a major gain would be only one additional drink. Drinking plenty of water is important for well-being and tends to fight cravings for food.

Week 2: Mindfulness

(Health micro-habit 2: Compose one sentence a day in your log).

By having just one extra glass of water every day before you hit eight glasses (64 ounces). Maintain your week 1 microhabitat of Wellness and notice the quantity of water you get in your record every day or by using the Health Habits Application.

You will continue to exercise mindfulness when the progress starts with balanced fuels. Focus on a moment per day when you had an urge and how you dealt with it, or journal about an achievement. One sentence is what it involves. Mindfulness allows you to take actions that take you further towards excellence. On your path, introducing this routine into your everyday life would give you an essential archive of your feelings and emotions.

Week 3: Evolve with Habits of Good Sleep

You are now consuming more water and writing every day. You are well on the way to introducing a new lifestyle pattern into your everyday life. The theme this week is good sleep. Rest is an underrated component of your overall well-being. It will alleviate discomfort, decrease food cravings, avoid overeating, and enhance performance by having seven to nine hours of tranquil nighttime sleep.

(Health micro-habit 3: Stop consuming caffeine after midday).

Your latest micro-habit of Wellness is to stop consuming coffee, tea, or other forms of caffeine after 1 PM every day. This tiny twick will get you more inclined to have a relaxing night's sleep. Also, it could render you more susceptible to caffeine and hold you much more alert at night by adopting a reduced-calorie food program.

Week 4: Develop the Habits of Healthy Movement

Strenuous exercise can do far more damage than good, particularly when you're not prepared. Eating nutritious fuels every two or three hours, consuming enough liquids, journal writing, sleeping well through having less coffee, and becoming mindful, creates a difference throughout your life. Now, once again, with this microhabitat of Wellness, you are beginning to be more active.

(Health 4 micro-habit: Stand for an additional one per day).

Standing up for your latest Television show or when reading a book is your fresh micro-habit of Wellness for the week. When you steady your stance, standing stimulates nearly every muscle in the body. It sounds insignificant but sitting down less is one of the greatest health tips in years, so an additional one hour of standing per day is a fine idea! Share with your friends and family this exercise to bring further activity into their lifestyles.

PART 1: LEAN AND GREEN RECIPES

APPETIZERS

Easy BBQ Meatballs

Ingredients:
- 5 Turkey Meatballs (1 Lean)
- 1/4 cup BBQ Sauce (2 Condiments)
- 1 tsp. low sodium soy sauce (1/2 Condiment)

Directions:
Follow the instructions to cook the meatballs. Combine BBQ sauce and soy sauce in a small bowl and pour over meatballs.

Servings: 2

Each serving provides 1 Lean, 2.5 Condiments

Buffalo Cauliflower Bites – Air Fryer

Ingredients:
- 5 1/2 cup cauliflower florets (9 Greens)
- 1/2 cup of hot sauce (4 Condiments)
- 1/4 tsp. garlic powder (1/2 Condiment)
- 6 tbsp. light ranch dressing (3 Healthy Fats)

Directions:

    27

Add 1/4 cup Hot Sauce and garlic powder to the cauliflower florets and toss. Place a piece of unwaxed parchment paper on the bottom of the air fryer. Set the air fryer to 360°F and cook for 12 to 15 minutes, shaking every 5 minutes. Add the remaining 1/4 cup of Hot Sauce to the cooked cauliflowers and serve with 2 tbsp. light ranch dressing

Servings: 3
Each serving provides 3 Greens, 1 1/2 Condiments, and 1 Healthy Fat.

Buffalo Chicken Bake

Ingredients:
- 9 oz. cooked chicken breasts, shredded or chopped (1 1/2 Leaner)
- 1/2 cup reduced-fat cheddar cheese (1/2 Lean)
- 1/4 cup Hot Wings Sauce (2 Condiments)
- 1/4 cup Light Ranch Dressing (2 Healthy Fats)
- 2 oz. reduced-fat cream cheese (4 Condiments)
- 6 Servings of Veggies (6 Greens)

Directions:
Preheat oven to 350 degrees. Mix together Hot Wings Sauce, ranch dressing, cream cheese, and chicken shreds. Toss to coat. If necessary heat the cream cheese a little bit. Pour the mixture on a baking tray with parchment paper, sprinkle the cheddar on top, and bake for 10 minutes.
Serve with 1 1/2 cups of veggies.

Servings: 2
Each serving provides 1 Leaner, 3 Greens, 3 Condiments, and 1 Healthy Fat

Cabbage Wrapped Beef Pot Stickers

Ingredients:
- 2 ½ oz. of cooked cabbage (1 Green)
- 8 oz. 95% to 97% Ground Beef raw (1 Leaner Lean)
- 2 tbsp. chopped green onion (1/4 Green)
- 1 tsp. Sesame oil (1 Healthy Fat)
- 1 tbsp. lite Soy sauce (1 Condiment)
- 1/8 tsp. Ground Ginger (1/4 Condiment)
- 1/8 tsp. Garlic Powder (1/4 Condiment)

Directions:
Wash and cut cabbage in half. Cut the core from each and separate 8 leaves. Boil them for 2 minutes and then drain them on a clean towel.
Combine beef, chopped green onions, sesame oil, soy sauce, ginger, and garlic powder in a mixing bowl. Make small patties from it and cook them on a pan with cooking spray over medium heat four minutes per side. Wrap them in cabbage leaves.

Servings: 1
Each serving provides 1 Leaner Lean, 1 Green, 1 Healthy Fat, and 1.5 Condiments

Caprese Spaghetti Squash Nests

Ingredients:
For the Nests:
- 2 cups cooked spaghetti squash (4 Greens)
- 1/4 tsp. salt (1 Condiment)
- 1/4 tsp. black pepper (1/2 Condiment)
- 1/4 tsp. garlic powder (1/2 Condiment)
- 3 tbsp. liquid egg whites (1 Condiment)

For the Filling:
- 1 cup cherry tomatoes (2 Greens)
- 1/4 tsp. salt (1 Condiment)
- 1/4 tsp. black pepper (1/2 Condiment)

- 4 oz. shredded reduced-fat Mozzarella cheese (1 Lean)
- 1/4 cup basil, chopped (1/2 Condiment)

Directions:
Oven Method for Spaghetti Squash:
Preheat oven to 375°F. Wash and cut in half the squash. Remove the seeds with a spoon. Place squash cut side down on a baking tray with parchment paper. Bake for 50 min. Let cool and shred the squash using a fork, forming noodles. Reserve 2 cups for this recipe.

Assembly of the nests:
Preheat oven to 400°F and spray a muffin pan with cooking spray. Combine the spaghetti squash with salt, pepper, egg whites, and garlic powder. Fill the muffin cups with the mixture (1/4 cup each) forming nests. Bake for 20 minutes.
In the meantime, on another baking tray with parchment paper, spread the cherry tomatoes cut in halves. Season them with salt and pepper and bake for 20 minutes together with the nests.
At the end of the baking, put the roasted cherry tomatoes in each nest, sprinkle 2 tbsp. of Mozzarella on to and bake 10 minutes more. Sprinkle fresh basil on top at the end.

Servings: 2 (4 Nests each)
Each serving provides 1/2 Lean, 3 Greens, and 2.5 Condiments

Cheese Stuffed Jalapenos

Ingredients:
- 2 light cream cheese (1 Healthy Fat)
- 1/4 cup 2% reduced-fat Mexican Three Cheese Blend (1/4 Lean)
- 1/8 tsp. Worcestershire sauce (1/4 Condiment)

- 3 to 4 Jalapenos, depends on size (1 Green)
- 2 tbsp. grated reduced-fat parmesan cheese (1 Condiment)

Directions:
Wash and cut jalapenos in half lengthwise, then remove the seeds. Boil them for 5 minutes, drain them, and set them aside. In the meantime, beat cream cheese, cheddar cheese, and Worcestershire sauce. Then fill the half peppers with two scoops of the mixture. Sprinkle with grated Parmesan cheese and place them on a baking tray with parchment paper. Bake in a preheated oven at 400°F F for 10 minutes.

Servings: 1
Each serving provides 1/4 Lean, 1 Green, 1.25 Condiments and 1 Healthy Fat

Cracker Shrimp

Ingredients:
- 11 ounces raw, peeled shrimp (1 Leanest)
- 2 tbsp. Apricot Preserves (2 Condiments)
- 1 tsp. lite soy sauce (1/3 Condiment)
- 1/2 tsp. sriracha sauce (1/2 Condiment)
- 1 tsp. sesame oil (1 Healthy Fat)

Directions:
Microwave the apricot preserves for 15 seconds until melted. Mix them with soy sauce, sriracha sauce, and oil to create the marinade. Put the shrimps in the bowl and let them marinate 1 hour in the fridge. Make skewers and grill them uncovered over high heat for two minutes on each side

Servings: 1
Each serving provides 1 Leanest, 3 Condiments, and 1 Healthy Fat

Grilled Buffalo Shrimp

Ingredients:
- 11 ounce raw, peeled, and cleaned shrimp (1 Lean)
- 1/4 cup Hot Sauce (2 Condiments)
- 1 tbsp. light butter (1 Healthy Fat)

Directions:
Melt the butter in the microwave and mix it with the hot sauce. Make shrimp skewers and brush them with the sauce. Grill the skewers 2 minutes on each side on high heat. Add the remaining buffalo sauce.
Servings: 1
Each serving provides 1 Lean, 2 Condiments, and 1 Healthy Fat

Grilled Chicken with Peanut Sauce

Ingredients:
- 12 oz. chicken tenderloins, grilled (2 Lean)
- For the sauce:
- 1/4 cup PB2 - Powdered Peanut Butter (2 Snacks)
- 1/4 tsp. garlic powder (1/2 Condiment)
- 1/2 tsp. ground ginger (1 Condiment)
- 1 tbsp. lite soy sauce (1 Condiment)
- 1 packet Stevia or Sweetener of choice (1 Condiment)
- 1 tbsp. apple cider vinegar (1/4 Condiment)
- Additional water
- 2 tsp. sesame oil (2 Healthy Fats)

Directions:
Combine all ingredients for the sauce. Stir until completely blended. Serve with chicken

Servings: 2
Each serving provides 1 Leaner, 2 Condiments, 1 Healthy Fat, and 1 Fueling

Italian Meatballs

Ingredients:
- 1 1/2 lbs. 95 to 97% lean ground beef or turkey (3 Leaner)
- 1/4 cup reduced-fat parmesan cheese (2 Condiments)
- 1 tsp. dried basil leaves (1/2 Condiment)
- 1/4 cup egg beaters (1 1/3 Condiments)
- 2 tbsp. fresh parsley (1/2 Condiment)
- 1/2 tsp. garlic powder (1 Condiment)
- 1/4 tsp. fresh black ground pepper (1/2 Condiment)
- 3/4 tsp. salt (3 Condiments)
- 3/4 cup marinara sauce, divided (3 Greens)

Directions:
Preheat oven to 400°F. Combine all the ingredients except the marinara sauce and mix them. Form meatballs and bake them for 22 minutes. Add ¼ cup of marinara sauce on top for each serving

Servings: 3
Each serving provides 1 Leaner, 1 Green, and 3 Condiments

Italian Zucchini Meatballs

Ingredients:
For the Meatballs
- 14 oz. 93% lean ground beef (2 Leans)
- 16 oz. Italian turkey sausage, casings removed* (2 Leans)
- 1 cup reduced-fat Mozzarella cheese (1 Lean)
- 6 tbsp. reduced-fat parmesan cheese (3 Condiments)
- 1 cup shredded zucchini (2 Greens)
- 3/4 tsp. salt (3 Condiments)
- 2 tsp. onion powder (4 Condiments)
- 2 tsp. fresh minced garlic (2 Condiments)
- 1 tsp. Italian seasoning (2 Condiments)
- 1 egg (1/3 Lean)

For the Topping
- 1 cup approved marinara sauce (4 Greens)
- 2/3 cup reduced-fat Mozzarella cheese (2/3 Lean)
- 1/4 cup fresh basil, chopped (1/4 Condiment)

Directions:
Preheat oven to 400 degrees. Shred the zucchini, squeeze them to remove the water, and place them on a clean towel. Combine all the ingredients for the meatballs and create meatballs. Place the balls on a baking tray with parchment paper. Bake them for 25 minutes, drain the excess grease, top with the marinara sauce and 2/3 cup of mozzarella. Bake 5 minutes more. Finish with fresh basil

Servings: 6
Each serving provides 1 Lean, 1 Green, and 2 1/2 Condiments

Quick and Easy Crock Pot Shredded Chicken

Ingredients:
- 3 pounds of chicken breasts or tenderloins (6 Leaner)
- 1 cup chicken broth (1 Condiment)
- Seasonings of choice ~ subtract from your Condiments

Directions:
Season the chicken. Place it in the slow cooker with chicken broth. Cook 6 to 8 hours on LOW and then drain the chicken. Shred with forks.

Servings: 6
Each serving provides 1 Leaner (Condiments will vary)

Baked Kale Chips

Ingredients:
- 4 1/2 cups kale leaves (9 Greens)
- 1 tbsp. olive oil (3 Healthy Fats)
- 1/4 tsp. sea salt (1 Condiment)

Directions:
Preheat oven to 350°F. Place the kale leaves, teared in 3-inch pieces, in a bowl and season them with salt and olive oil. Place the mix on a baking tray with parchment paper on a single layer. Bake for 10 minutes, turning them halfway through. You can vary the seasoning by adding paprika, garlic, parmesan cheese…

Servings: 3
Each serving provides 3 Greens, 1/3 of a Condiment and 1 Healthy Fat

Ricotta and Bacon Stuffed Mini Peppers

Ingredients:
- 18 mini peppers (6 Greens)
- 2/3 cup part-skim ricotta cheese (2/3 Lean)
- 1 egg, beaten (1/3 Lean)
- 1/2 cup reduced-fat Mozzarella cheese, shredded (1/2 Lean)
- 1/4 cup freshly grated parmesan cheese (4 Condiments)
- 4 slices turkey bacon (1/2 Lean)
- 2 tbsp. fresh basil chopped (1/4 Condiment)
- 2 tbsp. fresh parsley, chopped (1/2 Condiment)
- 1/4 tsp. salt (1 Condiment)
- 1/8 tsp. black pepper (1/4 Condiment)

Directions:
Preheat oven to 350°F. Grill the turkey bacon and chop it finely. Wash and cut peppers in half lengthwise, then remove seeds. Combine ricotta, egg, mozzarella,

parmesan, bacon chops, spices and fill the pepper with the mixture. Place the peppers on a baking tray with parchment paper and bake for 20 minutes.

Servings: 2
Each serving provides 1 Lean, 3 Greens, and 3 Condiments (about 18 pepper halves)

Taco Cups

Ingredients:
- 2 slices reduced-fat cheese slices (1/2 Lean)
- 3 oz. cooked 95 to 97% lean ground beef (1/2 Lean)
- 1 tsp. taco seasoning (2 Condiments)

Directions:
Preheat oven to 375°F. Combine the meat with taco seasoning.
On a muffin tin sprayed with cooking spray, line the cheese slices and bake them for 5 minutes. Let it cool to obtain a cheese cup and carefully remove them from the tray. Fill the cups with the meat and enjoy.

Servings: 1
Each serving provides 1 Lean and 2 Condiments

Taco Meatballs and Cheese Appetizers

Ingredients:
- 12 oz. cooked 95 to 97% ground beef (2 Leaner Leans)
- 1/4 cup egg beaters (1/8 Lean)
- 1 tbsp. taco seasoning mix (6 Condiments)
- 1/4 cup cilantro, chopped (1/4 Condiment)
- 3.5 oz. 2% fat Cheddar Cubes (7/8 Lean)

Dip:
- 1/4 cup sour cream (2 Healthy Fats)
- 2 tbsp. salsa (2 Condiments)

Directions:
Mix in a bowl ground beef, eggbeaters, cilantro, and taco seasoning. Form meatballs and place them on a baking tray with parchment paper. Bake at 425 degrees for 15 minutes. Combine sour cream and salsa.
Serve the meatballs with salsa and cheese cubes

Servings: 3
Each serving provides 1 Leaner Lean, 2.75 Condiments and 1 Healthy Fat

Zucchini Chips

Ingredients:
- 1 1/2 cups zucchini slices (3 Greens)
- 1 teaspoon olive oil (1 Healthy Fat)
- 1/8 tsp. sea salt (1/4 Condiment)

Directions:
Preheat oven to 200°F. Mix in a bowl the zucchini slices with salt and oil. Line them on a baking sheet with parchment paper on a single layer. Bake 3 hours, turning them occasionally

Servings: 3
Each serving provides 1 Green, 1/3 Healthy Fat, and 1/12 Condiment

Taco Zucchini Boats

Preparation Time: 20 minutes
Cooking Time: 40 minutes
Servings: 4

Ingredients:
- 4 medium zucchinis (cut in half lengthwise)

- ¼ cup fresh cilantro (chopped)
- ½ cup cheddar cheese (shredded)
- ¼ cup of water
- 4 oz. tomato sauce
- 2 tbsp. bell pepper (mined)
- ½ small onion (minced)
- ½ tsp. oregano
- 1 tsp. paprika
- 1 tsp. chili powder
- 1 tsp. cumin
- 1 tsp. garlic powder
- 1 lb. lean ground turkey
- ½ cup of salsa
- 1 tsp. kosher salt

Directions:
1) Preheat the oven to 400° F.
2) Add ¼ cup of salsa in the bottom of the baking dish.
3) Use a spoon hollow out the center of the zucchini halves.
4) Chop the scooped-out flesh of zucchini and set aside ¾ of a cup chopped flesh.

5) Add zucchini halves in the boiling water and cook for 1 minute. Remove zucchini halves from water.
6) Add ground turkey in a large pan and cook until meat is no longer pink. Add spices and mix well.
7) Add reserved zucchini flesh, water, tomato sauce, bell pepper, and onion. Stir well and cover, simmer over low heat for 20 minutes.
8) Stuff zucchini boats with taco meat and top each with one tablespoon of shredded cheddar cheese.
9) Place zucchini boats in baking dish. Cover dish with foil and bake in preheated oven for 35 minutes.
10) Top with remaining salsa and chopped cilantro.

Nutrition: Calories 297; 1 Leanest protein, 2 Green

MEATS

Jambalaya

Ingredients:
- 1 link of Andouille Sausage, sliced (1/2 Lean)
- 3 oz. Chicken, cooked (1/2 Lean)
- 1/4 cup Green Peppers, chopped (1/2 Green)
- 1/4 cup Celery, chopped (1/2 Green)
- 1 cup Canned, Diced Tomatoes (2 Greens)
- 1/4 cup Water
- 1/4 tsp. Paprika (1/2 Condiment)
- 1/4 tsp. dried Oregano (1/4 Condiment)
- 1/4 tsp. dried Thyme (1/4 Condiment)
- 1/4 tsp. Garlic Salt (1 Condiment)

Directions:
Cook in a skillet over medium heat, green peppers, and celery in olive oil until tender. Add the chicken, tomatoes, water and spices. Cook until most of the liquid is boiled off. Stir in sausage bits

Servings: 1
Each serving provides 1 Lean, 3 Greens, 2 Condiments

Mexican Style Shredded Pork

Ingredients:
- 28 oz. pork loin roasted (4 Leans)
- 1/2 tsp. salt (2 Condiments)

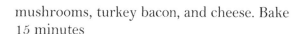
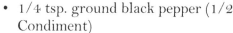

- 1/4 tsp. ground black pepper (1/2 Condiment)
- 1/4 tsp. garlic powder (1/2 Condiment)
- 1/2 tsp. chili powder (1 Condiment)
- 2 - 4 oz. cans of green chilies (2 Greens)
- 1/2 cup chipotle salsa (8 Condiments)
- 1/2 cup water

Directions:
Rinse the pork loin and pat it dry with kitchen paper. Cut away all the visible fat and season with salt, pepper, chili powder, and garlic powder. Place in the slow cooker with green chilies, salsa, and water. Cook on LOW for 8 hours. Then shred the pork and cook on LOW for an additional 1 hour.

Servings: 4
Each serving provides 1 Lean, 1/2 of 1 Green, and 3 Condiments

Springs Chicken

Ingredients:
- 1 ½ lb. raw chicken breasts
- 8 slices turkey bacon, cooked
- 1 cup reduced-fat cheddar cheese, shredded
- ¾ tsp. seasoned salt (3 Condiments)
- ½ tsp. black pepper (1 Condiment)
- ¾ cup Mustard Sauce, divided (6 Condiments)
- 2 cups mushrooms, sliced (4 Greens)
- 2 tablespoon light butter (2 Healthy Fats)

Directions:
Preheat oven to 380°F. Season the chicken with salt and pepper and place it in a Ziploc bag with half a cup of honey mustard. Marinate in the fridge for 2 hours. Put the butter in a hot skillet and cook the mushrooms for 5 minutes. After removing the chicken from the marinade, place it in a hot skillet sprayed with Pam. Cook 5 minutes per side, then move it in a 9x9 casserole. Top it with 1 tbsp. mustard, mushrooms, turkey bacon, and cheese. Bake 15 minutes

Servings: 4
Each serving provides 1 Lean, 1 Green, 3 Condiments, and ½ Healthy Fat

Almond Maple Chicken

Ingredients:
- 6 oz. cooked chicken breasts (1 Leaner Lean)
- 2 tbsp. pancake syrup (1/2 Condiment)
- 1/2 tbsp. grated fresh lemon zest (1/2 Condiment)
- 1 teaspoon lemon juice (1/2 Condiment)
- 1/4 tsp. salt (1 Condiment)
- 1/8 tsp. pepper (1/4 Condiment)
- 10 chopped almonds (1 Fueling)

Directions:
Heat oven to 400 °F. Put the chicken in a shallow baking pan and season it with salt, and pepper. Mix the syrup, lemon zest and pour it on the chicken. Cover with chopped almonds. Bake for 30 minutes.

Servings: 1
Each serving provides 1 Leaner Lean, 2.75 Condiments and 1 Fueling

Chicken with Mushroom Cream Sauce

Ingredients:
- For the Chicken
- 8 oz. chicken breasts (1 Leaner Lean)
- 1/4 tsp. salt (1 Condiment)
- 1/8 tsp. pepper (1/4 Condiment)
- 1/4 tsp. garlic powder (1/2 Condiment)

For the Sauce
- 1/2 cup mushrooms (1 Green)
- 1 scallion, thinly sliced

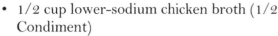

- 1/2 cup lower-sodium chicken broth (1/2 Condiment)
- 2 tbsp. reduced-fat cream cheese (1 Healthy Fat)
- 1/2 tbsp. fresh rosemary, chopped (1/4 Condiment)

Directions:
Cook on a non-stick skillet, sprayed with cooking spray, the chicken with its seasoning until cooked. When it is ready remove it from heat and cover it with tin foil to keep it warm. In the same skillet, spray some cooking spray and add the mushrooms. Cook them for 4 minutes, and then add broth, cream cheese, and rosemary. Let it cook one minute more whisking to melt the cheese. Put the chicken in the pan and bring to a simmer. Cook for some more minutes to reach a creamy texture.

Servings: 1
Each serving provides 1 Leaner Lean, 1 Green, 2 1/2 Condiments, and 1 Healthy Fat

Chicken Teriyaki

Ingredients
- 2 teaspoons olive oil (2 Healthy Fats)
- 1/4 cup lite soy sauce (4 Condiments)
- 1/2 teaspoon onion powder (1 Condiment)
- 1/4 teaspoon garlic powder (1/2 Condiment)
- 1/4 tsp. ground ginger (1/2 Condiment)
- 16 oz. chicken breasts, boneless and skinless (2 Leaner Leans)

Directions:
Combine all the ingredients and marinate the chicken overnight. Discard marinade and grill chicken 5 minutes on each side.

Servings: 1
Each serving provides 1 Leaner Lean, 3 Condiments, and 1 Healthy Fat

Cilantro Lime Chicken and Zucchini Noodles

Ingredients:
- 1.5 pounds of boneless, skinless chicken breasts, chopped in 1" cubes (3 Leaner Leans)
- 4 1/2 cups spiralized zucchini noodles (9 Greens)
- 1/4 tsp. garlic salt (1 Condiment)
- 1/4 tsp. fresh ground black pepper (1/2 Condiment)
- 2 tsp. taco seasoning (4 Condiments)
- 2 tbsp. lime juice (3 Condiments)
- 1/2 cup fresh cilantro, chopped (1/2 Condiment)
- 4 1/2 oz. avocado, diced (3 Healthy Fats)

Directions:
Cook the chicken in a skillet sprayed with Pam to medium-high heat. Add taco seasoning and cook for 8 minutes. Remove the chicken from the skillet and set it aside. Spray the skillet with Pam again and return to the heat. Add the zucchini noodles and cook for 1 minute. Pour the chicken bites in the skillet again and add lime juice, salt, pepper and cilantro. Remove from heat and serve with 1 1/2 oz. of diced avocado to each serving.

Servings: 3
Each serving provides 1 Lean, 3 Greens, 3 Condiments and 1 Healthy Fat

Grilled Turkey and Cheddar "Sandwich"

Ingredients:
- 2 cups grated cauliflower (4 Greens)
- 1 egg (1/3 Lean)

- 1/4 cup grated reduced-fat Parmesan cheese (2 Condiments)
- 1/4 tsp. dried Italian seasoning (1/2 Condiment)
- 2/3 cup shredded 2% sharp cheddar cheese (2/3 Lean)
- 6 ounces thinly sliced turkey breast (1 Lean)

Directions:
Mix until evenly combined grated cauliflower, egg, Parmesan cheese, and Italian seasonings. In the meantime, heat a large non-stick skillet sprayed with Pam. Create 4 small patties from the cauliflower mix and cook them in the skillet about 4 minutes per side. These are the "bread" part of our sandwiches. Assembly the sandwich with 1/3 cup cheese and 3 ounces of turkey. Cook in the skillet until cheese is melted, for about 2 minutes more per side.

Servings: 2
Each serving provides 1 Lean, 2 Greens, and 1.25 Condiments per Sandwich

Grilled Balsamic Marinated Chicken

Ingredients:
- 16 oz. raw boneless, skinless chicken breasts (2 Lean)

Marinade:
- 1 teaspoon dried basil (1/2 Condiment)
- 1/4 tsp. garlic powder (1/2 Condiment)
- 1/4 teaspoon black pepper (1/2 Condiment)
- 1/4 teaspoon salt (1 Condiment)
- 1/4 cup Balsamic Vinaigrette (2 Healthy Fats)

Directions:
Mix all ingredients in bowl and marinate chicken overnight. Grill chicken, drained from marinade, ten minutes.

Servings: 2
Each serving provides 1 Leaner Lean, 1.25 Condiments, and 1 Healthy Fat

Mashed Potato "Buns"

Ingredients:
- 1 Branded Mashed Potatoes (1 Fueling)
- 2 Egg Whites (1/7 Lean)
- 1 tsp. Baking Powder (2 Condiments)

Directions:
Preheat oven to 350°F. Whisk the egg whites until foamy, add baking powder and mashed potatoes. Combine the ingredients and pour the mixture into a Ziploc bag. Shape the bread into the desired shape. Put the bread on a baking tray with parchment paper and bake for 12 minutes.

Servings: 1
Each serving provides 1 Fueling, 1/7 Leanest and 2 Condiments

Chicken Parmesan

Ingredients:
- 32 oz. raw boneless, skinless chicken breasts (4 Leans)
- 2 cups crushed tomatoes (4 Greens)
- 1/2 tsp. Italian Seasoning (1 Condiment)
- 1 tsp. Basil (1/2 Condiment)
- 1/4 tsp. Onion Powder (1/2 Condiment)
- 2 cloves garlic (2 Condiments)
- 2 tbsp. Grated Reduced-fat Parmesan Cheese (1 Condiment)

Directions:
Place chicken in a slow cooker with the other ingredients. Cook on low 6 hours. Serve with 1/2 cup sauce.

Servings: 4
Each serving provides 1 Leaner Lean, 1 Green, and 1.25 Condiments

Maple Orange Glazed Chicken

Ingredients:
- 18 oz. raw boneless, skinless chicken breasts - should yield 12 oz. cooked (2 Lean)
- 2 tbsp. Maple Syrup (1 condiment)
- 1 tablespoon Orange Marmalade (1 condiment)
- 2 teaspoons Balsamic Vinegar (2 condiments)
- 1 teaspoon Dijon Mustard (1 condiment)
- 1 teaspoon Basil (1 condiment)
- 2 teaspoons Olive Oil (2 Healthy Fats)

Directions:
Cook the chicken in a hot non-stick skillet over medium-high heat. Discard oil in the pan and place over medium heat. Add maple syrup, marmalade, balsamic vinegar, Dijon mustard, and basil. Thicken the sauce for 1 minute and pour it over the chicken.

Servings: 2
Each serving provides 1 Lean, 3 Condiments, and 1 Healthy Fat

Orange Chicken

Ingredients:
- 1 can diet orange soda
- 1/4 cup lite soy sauce (4 Condiments)
- 1 tablespoon teriyaki sauce (3 Condiments)
- 1/2 teaspoon crushed red pepper (1 Condiment)
- 1 cloves garlic, minced (1 Condiment)
- 1/4 tsp. ground ginger (1/2 Condiment)
- 32 oz. raw, boneless, skinless chicken breasts (4 Leaner Leans)

Directions:
Pierce chicken breasts several times with a fork. In a Ziploc bag put together all the ingredients and let the chicken marinate overnight in the fridge. Lastly, drain the chicken and grill it.

Servings: 4
Each serving provides 1 Lean and 2.3 Condiments

Rotisserie Style Chicken

Ingredients:
- 1 tsp. salt (4 Condiments)
- 1 tsp. paprika (2 Condiments)
- 1/2 tsp. onion powder (1 Condiment)
- 1/2 tsp.. dried thyme (1/2 Condiment)
- 1/4 tsp. cayenne pepper (1/2 Condiment)
- 1/4 tsp. black pepper (1/2 Condiment)
- 1/4 tsp. garlic powder (1/2 Condiment)
- 4 lb. chicken

Directions:
Mix all the spices together and rub the chicken with it. Be careful to rub also under the skin. Put it inside a Ziploc bag and marinate it overnight.
Preheat oven to 275°F. Bake the chicken uncovered for about 4 hours. Let the chicken rest for 10 minutes before slicing.

Servings: 4
Each serving provides 1 Lean, 2.25 Condiments

Slow Cooker Cashew Chicken

Ingredients:
- 24 oz. raw chicken breasts cut into 1-inch pieces (3 Leaner)

Sauce:
- 1/4 cup lite soy sauce (4 Condiments)
- 2 tbsp. reduced sugar ketchup (2 Condiments)
- 2 tbsp. rice wine vinegar (1/2 Condiment)

- 1 packet of stevia or sweetener of choice (1 Condiment)
- 1 tsp. minced garlic (1 Condiment)
- 1/4 tsp. ground ginger (1/2 Condiment)

Garnish:
- 1 oz. cashews, chopped (3 Healthy Fats)

Directions:
Cook the chicken until well brown in a hot skillet sprayed with Pam. Season it with salt and pepper. Add chicken to the slow cooker with the sauce ingredients. Cook on LOW for 3 hours. Garnish with 1/3 ounce of chopped cashews and sliced green onions per serving. Serve immediately. Enjoy!

Servings: 3
Each serving provides 1 Leaner, 3 Condiments, and 1 Healthy Fat

Asian Beef Vegetable Skewers

Ingredients:
- 14 oz. raw beef sirloin cut into 1-inch pieces (2 Leans)

Marinade for Meat:
- 1/4 cup lite soy sauce (4 Condiments)
- 1 tsp. beef bouillon granules (1 Condiment)
- 1/4 cup water
- 1/2 tsp. garlic powder (1 Condiment)
- 1/2 tsp. ground ginger (1 Condiment)
- 1/4 tsp. black pepper (1/2 Condiment)

Vegetables:
- 1 cup sliced yellow squash (2 Greens)
- 1 cup cherry tomatoes (2 Greens)
- 1 cup green pepper, cut into 1 inch pieces (2 Greens)

Directions:
Marinate the meat with the marinade ingredients in a Ziploc bag overnight. Add veggies to marinate one hour before

cooking. Drain meat and vegetables and assemble the skewers with meat and vegetables. Grill 5 minutes per side

Servings: 2
Each serving provides 1 Lean, 3 Greens and 2 Condiments

Beef Pad Thai

Ingredients:
- 3 1/2 cups cooked spaghetti squash (7 Greens)
- 1 cup shredded red cabbage, (2 Greens)
- 18 ounces Beef Steak Strips (3 Leaner)

For the sauce
- 1/4 cup reduced-sodium beef broth (1/4 Condiment)
- 1/4 cup Powdered Peanut Butter (2 Fuelings)
- 1 tbsp. rice wine vinegar (1/4 Condiment)
- 2 tbsp. light soy sauce (2 Condiments)
- 1/8 tsp. red cayenne pepper (1/4 Condiment)
- 1/4 tsp. ground ginger (1/2 Condiment)
- 1/2 tsp. garlic powder (1 Condiment)

Directions:
Make holes on all sides of the squash. Microwave the squash wrapped in a paper towel, on high for 3 minutes at a time until soft. Let cool and cut in half, lengthwise. Remove seeds with a scoop and scrape the squash with a fork until you reach the skin. You will need 3 1/2 cups of spaghetti squash for this recipe. Cook 6 minutes the thawed beef steak strips into a skillet over medium-high heat. In the meantime, prepare the sauce combining all the ingredients. Cook spaghetti squash, cabbage, and sauce in a skillet for 5 minutes

Servings: 3

Each serving provides 1 Leaner, 3 Greens, 1 1/2 Condiments, and 2/3 Fueling

Carne Guisada

Ingredients:
- 28 oz. chuck roast, trimmed and cubed (4 Lean)
- 1/2 cup chopped green chilies (1 Green)
- 1 1/2 cups canned, diced tomatoes, undrained (3 Greens)
- 2 cups beef broth (2 Condiments)
- 1 oz. jarred jalapeno, chopped (1 Condiment)
- 1 tbsp. chili powder (3 Condiments)
- 1/4 tsp. garlic powder (1/2 Condiment)
- 1 tsp. onion powder (2 Condiments)
- 1 tsp. cumin (1 Condiment)
- 1/4 tsp. salt (1 Condiment)
- 1/2 tsp. pepper (1 Condiment)

Directions:
Add all of the ingredients into a crock-pot. Cook on low 8 to 10 hours.

Servings: 4
Each serving provides 1 Lean, 1 Green, and 3 Condiments.

Inside Outside Egg Rolls

Ingredients:
- 1 cup cabbage shredded (2 Greens)
- 1/4 cup celery, chopped (1/2 Green)
- 1/4 cup scallions, chopped (1/2 Green)
- 7 oz. raw 93% lean ground beef (1 Lean)
- 1/4 cup egg beaters (1/8 Lean)
- 1/8 tsp. ground ginger (1/4 Condiment)
- 1/8 tsp. garlic powder (1/4 Condiment)
- 1/8 tsp. Chinese five spice blend (1/4 Condiment)
- 1 tbsp. lite soy sauce (1 Condiment)

Directions:
Combine shredded cabbage, celery, and scallions and set aside. Cook ground beef in a skillet and add the veggies. Sprinkle the spices, add soy sauce, and egg beaters. Continue to cook until vegetables are tender.

Servings: 1
Each serving provides 1 Lean, 3 Greens, and 1.75 Condiments

Meatloaf

Ingredients:
- 28 oz. raw 93% lean ground beef (4 Leans)
- 1/4 cup eggbeaters
- 1 cup low sugar tomato sauce, divided (4 Greens)
- 1/2 cup reduced-fat grated parmesan cheese (4 Condiments)
- 2 tbsp. lite soy sauce (2 Condiments)
- 1/2 tsp. garlic powder (1 Condiment)
- 2 tsp. onion powder (4 Condiments)
- 1 tbsp. dried parsley (1 Condiment)

Directions:
Preheat oven to 350°F. Mix ground all the ingredients except ¼ of low sugar tomato sauce. Put the mix in a baking tray with parchment paper and bake for 1 hour.
Finish with the remaining tomato sauce and bake for 10 minutes more. Drain the fat and serve.

Servings: 4
Each serving provides 1 Lean, 1 Green, and 3 Condiments

Meat Lasagna

Ingredients:
- 10 oz. 93% ground beef, cooked (2 Leans)
- 1 cup Rao's marinara sauce (4 Greens)

 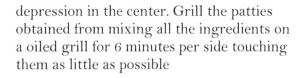

- 1/4 tsp. garlic powder (1/2 Condiment)
- 1/4 tsp. salt (1 Condiment)
- 1/8 tsp. pepper (1/4 Condiment)

Cheese Filling:
- 4 oz. or 1/2 cup part-skim ricotta cheese (1/2 Leaner Lean)
- 6 oz. or 1 1/2 cups reduced-fat Mozzarella cheese, divided (1 1/2 Leans)
- 1/4 cup reduced-fat parmesan cheese (2 Condiments)
- 2 tbsp. eggbeaters
- 1/4 tsp. garlic powder (1/2 Condiment)
- 1 tsp. Italian Seasoning (2 Condiments)
- 1/8 tsp. pepper (1/4 Condiment)

Directions:
Preheat oven to 350 °F. Mix together marinara sauce, garlic powder, salt, pepper, and ground beef and let it in a pan for 5 minutes. Mix the cheese filling ingredients. In a baking tray put the meat and the cheese filling, bake for 40 minutes, and serve after 10 minutes rest.

Servings: 4
Each serving provides 1 Lean, 1 Green (Still need 2 Greens), and 1.6 Condiments

Perfect Burger

Ingredients:
- 1 ½ lbs. 93% lean ground beef
- 1 egg
- 1 tsp. prepared mustard (1/3 Condiment)
- 1 tsp. Worcestershire sauce (2 Condiments)
- ¼ tsp. garlic powder (1/2 Condiment)
- ¼ tsp. onion powder (1/2 Condiment)
- ½ tsp. salt (2 Condiments)
- ½ tsp. black pepper (1 Condiment)

Directions:
Mix all the ingredients and create patties ¾ inches thick. Using your thumb create a

depression in the center. Grill the patties obtained from mixing all the ingredients on a oiled grill for 6 minutes per side touching them as little as possible

Servings: 4
Each serving provides 1 Lean and 1.5 Condiments

Philly Cheesesteak Stuffed Peppers

Ingredients:
- 4 medium green bell peppers
- 1/3 cup diced yellow onion
- 2 tsp. minced garlic
- ¼ cup low sodium beef broth
- 6 oz. sliced mushrooms
- 1 lb. thinly sliced steak
- 4 tbsp. low-fat cream cheese
- 4 oz. reduced-fat provolone cheese, sliced

Directions:
Preheat oven to 400°F. Cut peppers in half by the length and remove seeds. In a skillet cook onions and garlic with the broth for about 5 min. Add the mushrooms and continue cooking for 5 more minutes. Add the roast beef now and cook for 5 more minutes. Remove from heat and add cream cheese. Fill each pepper half with the mixture and top with 1/2oz. cheese. Bake 20 minutes

Servings: 4
Each serving provides 1 Lean, 3 Greens, and 3 Condiments

Shepard's pie

Ingredients:
- 7.5 oz. cooked 93% lean ground beef (1 1/2 Leans)
- 1 tbsp. gravy mix (4 Condiments)
- 1/4 cup water

- 1 1/2 cups drained canned green beans (3 Greens)
- 1/4 tsp. salt (1 Condiment)
- 1/8 tsp. black pepper (1/4 Condiment)
- 1/4 tsp. garlic powder (1/2 Condiment)
- 1 1/2 cups (9.51 oz.) cooked from frozen cauliflower, mashed (3 Greens)
- 1/2 cup shredded reduced-fat cheddar cheese (1/2 Lean)

Directions:
Preheat oven to 350°F. Combine cooked ground beef, gravy mix, water, and green beans in a medium pan and bring to a boil. Simmer 5 to 10 minutes. Let it Spread ground beef and green bean mixture on the bottom of a small casserole dish. Sprinkle cheese on top and bake for 30 minutes.

Servings: 4
Each serving provides 1 Lean, 3 Greens, and 3 Condiments

Simple Pot Roast

Ingredients:
- 2 lbs. 10 oz. chuck roast (6 Leans)
- 1 tsp. kosher salt (4 Condiments)
- 1/2 tsp. pepper (1 Condiment)
- 1/2 tsp. garlic powder (1 Condiment)
- 1 tsp. Italian seasoning (2 Condiments)
- 2 cups beef broth or 1 can (2 Condiments)

Directions:
Cut away all the visible fat from the roast and season it with salt, pepper, and garlic powder on all sides. Place the roast in the slow cooker with broth and Italian seasoning. Cover and cook on low for 8 to 9 hours.
Servings: 6
Each serving provides 1 Lean and 1.6 Condiments

Simple Beef with Broccoli Stir Fry

Ingredients:
- 14 oz. raw beef round steak, cut into strips (2 Leans)
- 3 tbsp. lite soy sauce (3 Condiments)
- 1 Stevia Packet (1 Condiment)
- 1/2 cup beef broth (1/2 Condiment)
- 1 clove garlic, minced (1 Condiment)
- 1/4 tsp. ground ginger (1/2 Condiment)
- 1 cup broccoli florets (2 Greens)
- 2 cups cooked, grated cauliflower (4 Greens)

Directions:
Marinade for 15 minutes the steak strips with soy sauce. Drain and stir fry the beef for about 5 minutes on high heat. Remove from pan and, add broccoli, broth, Stevia, garlic, and ginger. Cover and cook for 5 minutes. Add beef back and serve.

Servings: 2
Each serving provides 1 Lean, 3 Greens and 3 Condiments

Unstuffed Cabbage Roll

Ingredients:
- 25 oz. 93% lean ground beef, cooked (5 Leans)
- 1/2 tsp. onion powder (1 Condiment)
- 1/2 tsp. garlic powder (1 Condiment)
- 4 cups cabbage, chopped (8 Greens)
- 2 cans diced tomatoes (7 Greens)
- 1 tbsp. cider vinegar (1/4 Condiment)
- 1/8 tsp. ground cinnamon (1/4 Condiment)
- 1/2 tsp. ground black pepper (1 Condiment)
- 1 tsp. sea salt (4 Condiments)
- 1 packet stevia - optional (1 Condiment)
- 1/2 cup water

Directions:
Combine all the ingredients into a large saucepan over medium-high heat. Simmer for half an hour.
Servings: 5
Each serving provides 1 Lean, 3 Greens, 1.7 Condiments

Taco Salad with Quest Chips

Ingredients:
- 4 ounces 95 to 97% uncooked lean ground beef (1/2 Leaner)
- 1/2 tsp. taco seasoning (1 Condiment)
- 1/2 cup or 90 g tomatoes, chopped (1 Green)
- 2 cups or 94 g lettuce, shredded (2 Greens)
- 1 bag Quest Protein Chips (1/2 Leaner)

Directions:
Cook ground beef in a skillet until brown. Drain the excess and return on the heat. Put in taco seasoning and cook 2 minutes more. Mix lettuce and tomatoes and toss in the cooled ground beef. Top with protein chips.

Servings: 1
Each serving provides 1 Leaner, 3 Greens, 1 Condiment

Sweet Sloppy Joes

Ingredients:
- 8.75 oz. 93% lean ground beef, cooked and drained of fat (1 and 3/4 Lean)
- 1/4 cup reduced-fat sharp cheddar cheese (1/4 Lean)

For the Sauce:
- 3 tbsp. reduced sugar ketchup (3 Condiments)
- 1 tbsp. yellow mustard (1 Condiment)

- 1/2 tbsp. apple cider vinegar (1/8 Condiment)
- 1 tbsp. pancake syrup (1/4 Condiment)
- 1/2 tsp. chili powder (1 Condiment)
- 1/8 tsp. salt (1/2 Condiment)

Directions:
Cook ground beef in a skillet until brown. Drain the excess and return on the heat. Prepare the sauce mixing all the ingredients and pour it on the beef. Stir and cook for 5 minutes. Top each portion with 2 tbsp. cheese.
Servings: 2
Each serving 1 Lean and 3 Condiments

Braised Collard Greens in Peanut Sauce with Pork Tenderloin

Preparation Time: 20 minutes
Cooking Time: 1 hour 12 minutes
Servings: 4

Ingredients:
- 2 cups of chicken stock
- 12 cups of chopped collard greens
- 5 tablespoon of powdered peanut butter
- 3 cloves of garlic (crushed)
- 1 teaspoon of salt
- ½ teaspoon of allspice
- ½ teaspoon of black pepper
- 2 teaspoon of lemon juice
- ¾ teaspoon of hot sauce
- 1 ½ lb. of pork tenderloin

Directions:
1) Get a pot with a tight-fitting lid and combine the collards with the garlic, chicken stock, hot sauce, and half of the pepper and salt. Cook on low heat for about 1 hour or until the collards become tender.
2) Once the collards are tender, stir in the all-spice, lemon juice and powdered peanut butter. Keep it warm.

3) Season the pork tenderloin with the remaining pepper and salt, and broil in a toaster oven for 10 minutes until you have an internal temperature of 145° F. Make sure to turn the tenderloin every 2 minutes to achieve an even browning all over. After that, you can take away the pork from the oven and allow it to rest for like 5 minutes.

Nutrition: Calories: 320; Each serving provides 1 healthy fat, 2 lean, 1 Green.

Tender Lamb Chops

Preparation Time: 10 minutes
Cooking Time: 6 hours
Servings: 8

Ingredients:
- 8 lamb chops
- ½ teaspoon dried thyme
- 1 onion (sliced)
- 1 teaspoon dried oregano
- 2 garlic cloves (minced)
- Pepper and salt

Directions:
1) Add sliced onion into the slow cooker.
2) Combine thyme, oregano, pepper, and salt. Rub over lamb chops.

3) Place lamb chops on a low-heat cooker and top it with garlic.
4) Pour ¼ cup water around the lamb chops.
5) Cover and cook on low heat for 6 hours.
6) Serve and enjoy.

Nutrition: Calories: 40; 1 serving lean protein, 1 Condiment.

Smoky Pork & Cabbage

Preparation Time: 10 minutes
Cooking Time: 8 hours
Servings: 6

Ingredients:
- 3 lbs. pork roast
- 1/2 cabbage head, chopped
- 1 cup of water
- 1/3 cup liquid smoke
- 1 tablespoon kosher salt

Directions:
1) Rub the pork with kosher salt and place it into the crockpot.
2) Pour liquid smoke over the pork and add water.
3) Cover and cook on low heat for 7 hours.
4) Remove pork from crockpot and add cabbage in the bottom of crockpot.
5) Place pork on top of the cabbage.
6) Cover again and cook for 1 more hour.
7) Shred pork with a fork and serve.

Nutrition: Calories: 484; 1 serving lean protein, 1 Green.

Philly Cheesesteak Stuffed Peppers

Preparation Time: 20 minutes
Cooking Time: 50 minutes
Servings: 4

Ingredients:
- 4 medium green bell peppers, sliced on top and seeded
- 1/3 cup diced yellow onion
- 2 cloves garlic (minced)
- ¼ cup low sodium bean broth
- 6 ounces baby Bella mushrooms (sliced)
- 1 pound shaved deli roast beef
- 4 tablespoons low-fat cream cheese
- 4 ounces reduced-fat provolone cheese

Directions:
1) Preheat the oven to 4000 F.
2) Set aside the bell pepper and make sure that they are clean inside.
3) In a skillet, sauté the onion and garlic in broth over medium flame for 5 minutes. Add the mushrooms and deli beef. Stir to cook everything.
4) Remove from skillet and stir in the cream cheese.
5) Line each of the bell pepper with a quarter slice of cheese. Fill an eighth with the roast beef mixture and top with cheese.
6) Place in the oven and bake for 20 minutes.

Nutrition: Calories: 486; 2 Greens, 2 healthy fat, 1 lean protein.

Mini Mac in a Bowl

Preparation Time: 20 minutes
Cooking Time: 40 minutes
Servings: 4

Ingredients:
- 2 tablespoons diced yellow onion
- 5 ounces 99% lean ground beef
- 2 tablespoons light "Thousand island" dressing
- 1/8 teaspoon white vinegar
- 1/8 teaspoon onion powder
- 3 cups shredded romaine lettuce
- 2 tablespoons reduced-fat cheddar cheese
- 1 teaspoon sesame seeds

Directions:
1) Heat a skillet over medium flame. Grease skillet with cooking spray.
2) Add the onion and sauté for 1 minute. Add the beef and cook until lightly browned.
3) Meanwhile, mix the island dressing, white vinegar, and onion powder. Set aside.
4) Assemble by topping the lettuce with ground beef. Sprinkle cheese on top and garnish with pickle slices and sesame seeds. Drizzle with sauce.

Nutrition: Calories: 416; 2 servings healthy fat, 1 serving lean protein, 1 Green.

Air-Fried Chicken Pie

Preparation Time: 10 minutes
Cooking Time: 30 minutes
Servings: 2

Ingredients:
- Puff pastry: 2 sheets
- Chicken thighs: 2 pieces (cut into cubes)
- One small onion (chopped)
- Small potatoes: 2 (chopped)
- Mushrooms: 1/4 cup

- Light soya sauce
- One carrot (chopped)
- Black pepper to taste
- Worcestershire sauce to taste
- Salt to taste
- Italian mixed dried herbs
- Garlic powder: a pinch
- Plain flour: 2 tbsp.
- Milk as required
- Melted butter

Directions:
1) In a mixing bowl, add light soya sauce and pepper add the chicken cubes and coat well.
2) In a pan over medium heat, sauté carrot, potatoes, and onion. Add some water, if required, to cook the vegetables.
3) Add the chicken cubes and mushrooms and cook them too.
4) Stir in black pepper, salt, Worcestershire sauce, garlic powder, and dried herbs.
5) When the chicken is cooked through, add some of the flour and mix well.
6) Add in the milk and let the vegetables simmer until tender.
7) Place one piece of puff pastry in the baking tray of the air fryer, poke holes with a fork.
8) Add on top the cooked chicken filling and eggs and puff pastry on top, with holes. Cut the excess pastry off. Glaze with oil spray or melted butter
9) Air-fry at 180° F, for six minutes or until it becomes golden brown.
10) Serve with microgreens.

Nutrition: calories 224; 1 lean protein, 1 healthy fat, 1 Green, 1 Condiment.

Seasoned Pork Chops

Preparation Time: 10 minutes
Cooking Time: 4 hours

Servings: 4

Ingredients:
- 4 pork chops
- 2 garlic cloves (minced)
- 1 cup chicken broth
- 1 tablespoon poultry seasoning
- 1/4 cup olive oil
- Pepper and salt

Directions:
1) In a bowl, whisk together olive oil, poultry seasoning, garlic, broth, pepper, and salt.
2) Pour olive oil mixture into the slow cooker then place pork chops into the crockpot.
3) Cover and cook on high heat for 4 hours.
4) Serve and enjoy.

Nutrition: Calories: 386; 2 servings lean protein, 1 serving healthy fat.

Air Fryer Grilled Chicken Recipe

Preparation Time: 30 minutes
Cooking Time:20 minutes
Servings: 3

Ingredients:
- Chicken tenders: 4 cups
- Marinade:
- Honey: 2 Tbsp.
- Olive oil: 1/4 cup
- White vinegar: 2 Tbsp.
- Water: 2 Tbsp.
- Half teaspoon salt
- Garlic powder: 1 tsp.
- Half teaspoon of paprika
- Onion powder: 1 tsp.
- Half teaspoon crushed red pepper

Directions:
1) In a mixing bowl, add all ingredients for the marinade and mix well.
2) Then add the chicken mix to coat. Cover with plastic wrap and marinate in the refrigerator for half an hour.
3) Put chicken tenders in the air fryer basket in one even layer.
4) Cook for 3 minutes at 390 0 F. flip the tenders over and cook for five minutes more or until chicken is completely cooked through.
5) Serve with the side of salad greens.

Nutrition: calories 230; 1 lean protein, 1 healthy fat, 1 Green.

Air-Fried Buttermilk Chicken

Preparation Time: 30 minutes
Cooking Time: 20 minutes
Servings: 6

Ingredients:
- Chicken thighs: 4 cups skin-on, bone-in
- Marinade:
- Buttermilk: 2 cups
- Black pepper: 2 tsp.
- Cayenne Pepper : 1 tps.
- Salt : 2 tsp.
- Seasoned Flour:
- Baking powder: 1 tbsp.

- All-purpose flour: 2 cups
- Paprika powder: 1 tbsp.
- Salt: 1 tsp.
- Garlic powder: 1 tbsp.

Directions:
1) Let the air fry heat at 180° C.
2) With a paper towel, pat dry the chicken thighs.
3) In a mixing bowl, add paprika, black pepper, salt and mix well; then add chicken pieces. Add buttermilk and coat the chicken well. Let it marinate for at least 6 hours.
4) In another bowl, add baking powder, salt, flour, pepper, and paprika. Put one by one of the chicken pieces and coat in the seasoning mix.
5) Spray oil on chicken pieces and place breaded chicken skin side up in air fryer basket in one layer, cook for 8 minutes, and then flip the chicken pieces cook for another ten minutes
6) Take out and serve with salad greens.

Nutrition: Cal 210; 2 Greens, 1 healthy fat, 1 lean protein.

Low Carb Parmesan Chicken Meatballs

Preparation Time: 10 minutes
Cooking Time: 12 minutes
Servings: 20

Ingredients:
- Pork rinds: half cup, ground
- Ground chicken: 4 cups
- Parmesan cheese: half cup
- Kosher salt: 1 tsp.
- Garlic powder: 1 tsp.
- One egg beat
- Paprika: 1 tsp.
- Pepper: half tsp.
- Breading

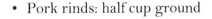

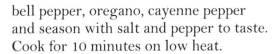

- Pork rinds: half cup ground

Directions:
1) Let the Air Fryer preheat to 400°F.
2) Add cheese, chicken, egg, and pepper, half cup of pork rinds, garlic, salt, and paprika in a big mixing ball. Mix well into a dough, make into 1and half-inch balls.
3) Coat the meatballs in pork rinds (ground).
4) Oil-spray the air fry basket and add meatballs in one even layer.
5) Let it cook for 12 minutes at 400°F, flipping once halfway through.
6) Serve with salad greens.

Nutrition: Cal 240; 2 lean protein, 1 healthy fat, 1 Green.

Mexican Turkey Soup

Preparation Time: 20 minutes
Cooking Time: 50 minutes
Servings: 4

Ingredients:
- ¼ cup olive oil
- 1 jalapeno (seeds removed then chopped)
- 1 cup cilantro (chopped)
- 2 cups green onions (finely chopped)
- 3 cloves garlic (minced)
- 1 cup red bell pepper (seeded and chopped)
- 1 teaspoon dried oregano
- ½ teaspoon cayenne pepper
- Salt and pepper to taste
- 12 ounces turkey breast (sliced)
- 6 Roma tomatoes (chopped)
- 2 cups chicken stock
- 2 cups tomato sauce

Directions:
1) Heat oil in a large pot and add the jalapeno, green onion, cilantro, garlic,

bell pepper, oregano, cayenne pepper and season with salt and pepper to taste. Cook for 10 minutes on low heat.
2) Add the turkey and cook for another 3 minutes before stirring in the tomatoes.
3) Add the remaining ingredients.
4) Bring to a boil for 10 minutes.
5) Remove from the heat and serve.

Nutrition: Calories: 427; 1 lean protein, 3 Green, 3 healthy fat.

Baked Chicken and Zucchini Casserole

Preparation Time: 20 minutes
Cooking Time: 40 minutes
Servings: 4

Ingredients:
- 1 ¾ pound boneless chicken breasts
- ¼ teaspoon garlic powder
- ¼ teaspoon salt
- ¼ teaspoon pepper
- 4 teaspoons olive oil
- 1 cup diced zucchini
- 1 cup diced tomatoes
- 1 teaspoon basil leaves
- 1 teaspoon oregano
- 1 cup part-skim mozzarella cheese

Directions:
1) Butter-fry the chicken slices in half to make four thin pieces.
2) Season with garlic powder, salt and pepper.
3) Heat the skillet over medium flame and add oil.
4) Brown the chicken slices in olive oil for 3 minutes on each side. Place the chicken in a baking dish. Set aside.
5) To the same skillet, sauté the zucchini in the pan until soft, then add the tomatoes, basil and oregano. Season it with more salt and pepper to taste.

6) Pour vegetable over chicken and top with mozzarella cheese.
7) Bake for 20 minutes in a 350°F preheated oven.
1) Nutrition: Calories: 373; 2 servings healthy fat, 1 serving leaner protein, 2 servings higher carb, 1 serving moderate carb.

Sriracha-Honey Chicken Wings

Preparation Time: 30 minutes
Cooking Time: 15 minutes
Servings: 2

Ingredients:
- Soy sauce: 1 and 1/2 tablespoons
- Chicken wings: 4 cups
- Sriracha sauce: 2 tablespoons
- Butter: 1 tablespoon
- Half cup honey
- Juice of half lime
- Scallion's cilantro and chives for garnish

Directions:
1) Let the air fryer preheat to 360° F.
2) Put the chicken wings to an air fryer basket, cook for half an hour, flip the wings every seven minutes, and cook thoroughly.

3) Meanwhile, in a saucepan, add all the ingredients of the sauce and simmer for three minutes.
4) Take out the chicken wings and coat them in sauce well.
5) Garnish with scallions. Serve with a microgreen salad.

Nutrition: Calories 207; 1 leaner protein, 1 healthy fat, 1 Condiment.

Italian Chicken Soup

Preparation Time: 20 minutes
Cooking Time: 50 minutes
Servings: 4

Ingredients:
- 1 lb. chicken breasts, boneless and cut into chunks
- 1 1/2 cups salsa
- 1 tsp. Italian seasoning
- 2 tbsp. fresh parsley (chopped)
- 3 cups chicken stock
- 8 oz. cream cheese
- Pepper and Salt

Directions:
1) Add all ingredients except cream cheese and parsley into the instant pot and stir well.
2) Seal pot and cook on high pressure for 25 minutes.
3) Release pressure using quick release. Remove lid.
4) Remove chicken from pot and shred using a fork.
5) Return shredded chicken to the instant pot.
6) Add cream cheese and stir well and cook on sauté mode until cheese is melted.
7) Serve and enjoy.

Nutrition: Calories 300; 1 leaner protein, 1 healthy fat, 1 Green.

Pesto Zucchini Noodles with Grilled Chicken

Preparation Time: 20 minutes
Cooking Time: 30 minutes
Servings: 4

Ingredients:
- 1/3 cup reduced-fat Italian salad dressing
- ½ cup chopped fresh basil
- ½ cup parmesan cheese (divided)
- 1/3 ounces pine nuts
- Cooking spray
- 2 medium zucchinis (paralyzed)
- 1 ½ pounds grilled boneless chicken breast (cubed)
- 2 cups cherry tomatoes (halved)
- ½ teaspoon crushed red pepper flakes

Directions:
1) Combine the salad dressing, basil, half of the parmesan cheese, and pine nuts. Then pulse in a blender until smooth.
2) In a lightly greased skillet heated over medium flame, cook the zucchini noodles for 3 minutes. Stir in the pesto and remaining parmesan cheese.
3) Remove from heat and top with chicken, tomatoes, and crushed red pepper flakes.

Nutrition: Calories: 335; 2 Greens, 1 leaner protein, 2 healthy fat, 1 Condiment.

Arroz Con Pollo

Preparation Time: 20 minutes
Cooking Time: 30 minutes
Servings: 4

Ingredients:
- 1 ¾ pound boneless chicken breasts
- ¼ teaspoon salt and pepper
- 2 cloves of garlic (minced)
- 1 scallion (minced)
- 4 cups cauliflower (grated)
- 1 ½ cups cherry tomato (halved)
- 40 green olives (pitted)
- ½ cup green beans cut into ¼ inch pieces

Directions:
1) Preheat the oven to 350 0 F.
2) Season the chicken with salt and pepper. Place on a greased baking sheet.
3) Roast the chicken for 20 minutes. Remove from the oven and set aside.
4) Meanwhile, mix all ingredients in a pot and simmer on low for 10 minutes.
5) Serve the cauliflower rice with the chicken.

Nutrition: Calories: 314; 2 Green, 1 leaner protein.

Chicken Casserole

Preparation Time: 20 minutes
Cooking Time: 60 minutes
Servings: 4

Ingredients:
- 1 lb. cooked chicken (shredded)
- ¼ cup Greek yogurt
- 1 cup cheddar cheese (shredded)
- ½ cup of salsa
- 4 oz. cream cheese (softened)
- 4 cups cauliflower florets
- 1/8 tsp. black pepper
- ½ tsp. kosher salt

Directions:

1) Add cauliflower florets into the microwave-safe dish and cook for 10 minutes or until tender.
2) Add cream cheese and microwave for 30 seconds more. Stir well.
3) Add chicken, yogurt, cheddar cheese, salsa, pepper, and salt then stir everything well.
4) Preheat the oven to 375° F.
5) Bake in preheated oven for 20 minutes.

Nutrition: Calories: 429; 3 servings lean protein, 1 Green.

SEAFOOD

Savory Salmon with Cilantro

Preparation Time: 20 minutes
Cooking Time: 25 minutes
Servings: 4

Ingredients:

- 4 cups fresh cilantro (divided)
- 2 tablespoons fresh lemon or lime juice
- 2 tablespoons red pepper sauce
- 1 teaspoon cumin
- ½ teaspoon salt
- ½ cup of water
- 4 to 7 ounces raw salmon filets

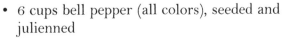 

- 6 cups bell pepper (all colors), seeded and julienned
- ½ teaspoon pepper
- Cooking spray

Directions:
1) Place half the cilantro, lemon juice, red pepper sauce, cumin, salt, and water in a blender. Pulse the blender until smooth. Transfer into a Ziploc bag and place the salmon. Marinate for 1 hour inside the fridge.
2) Pre-heat the oven to 400F. Arrange the bell peppers in a lightly greased baking dish. Sprinkle with pepper and bake for 10 minutes.
3) Drain the salmon and place on top the pepper slices and bake for 20 minutes.
4) Garnish with the remaining cilantro.

Nutrition: Calories: 341; 1 lean protein, 3 Greens

Garlic Tilapia

Ingredients:
- 9 oz. tilapia (1 Lean)
- 2 tsp. olive oil (2 Healthy Fats)
- 1 clove garlic, sliced (1 Condiment)
- 1/4 garlic and herb seasoning (1/2 Condiment)
- 1/8 tsp. black pepper (1/4 Condiment)
- 2 tsp. fresh lemon juice (1 Condiment)
- 1 tbsp. fresh parsley (1/4 Condiment)

Directions:
Season tilapia with the seasoning and pepper and cook in a skillet with the 2 tbsp. oil. After 2 minutes of cooking, add garlic slices and cook 4 more minutes. Flip the tilapia and cook 2 minutes more. Be careful to not burn the garlic. If it begins to burn, put it on the fish. Once cooked, finish with lemon juice and parsley

Servings: 1
Each serving provides 1 Lean Serving with 3 Condiments and 2 Healthy Fats

Middle Eastern Salmon with Tomatoes and Cucumber

Preparation Time: 20 minutes
Cooking Time: 35 minutes
Servings: 4

Ingredients:
- 4 cups sliced cucumber
- 1-pint cherry tomatoes halved
- ¼ cup cider vinegar
- ½ cup fresh dill (chopped)
- Salt and pepper to taste
- 1 ½ pounds skinless salmon
- 1 tablespoon Za'atar sauce
- 4 lemon wedges for garnish

Directions:
1) Preheat the oven to 350°F
2) Place the cucumber and tomatoes in a bowl. Add in the vinegar, dill, and season with salt and pepper to taste. Toss to coat.
3) Season the salmon with Za'atar on both sides and place in a foil-lined baking

sheet. Roast until the internal temperature reaches to 145° F.

4) Serve the roasted salmon with the cucumber and tomatoes.

Nutrition: Calories: 282; 1 lean protein, 3 Greens, 1 Condiment.

Salmon Florentine

Preparation Time: 10 minutes
Cooking Time: 30 minutes
Servings: 2

Ingredients:
- ½ cup chopped green onion
- 1 teaspoon olive oil
- 2 garlic cloves (minced)
- 1 12 oz. packaged frozen chopped spinach
- 1 ½ cups chopped celery
- ¼ teaspoon crushed red pepper flakes
- Salt and pepper to taste
- ½ cup part-skim ricotta cheese
- 5 ½ ounces wild salmon filets

Directions:
1) Preheat the oven to 350° F.
2) Heat skillet over medium flame and cook the green onions and olive oil. Add the garlic and cook for another 30 seconds. Stir in the spinach, celery, red pepper flakes, and season with salt and pepper to taste. Stir for 3 minutes until the spinach has wilted. Turn off the heat and set aside to cool slightly.
3) Mix the ricotta cheese into the cooked spinach. Mix until it's well-combined.
4) Place the salmon on a parchment-lined baking sheet. Top the salmon with the ricotta and spinach mixture.
5) Place in the oven for 30 minutes.

Nutrition: Calories: 145; 2 lean protein, 1 Green, 2 Healthy Fats

Thai Curry Shrimp

Ingredients:
- 1 tsp. oil (1 Healthy Fat)
- 9 oz. shrimp, peeled and deveined (1 Leanest Lean)
- 2 tsp. Thai green curry paste - 3 g of Carbs per tbsp. (2 Condiments)
- 1/8 tsp. garlic powder (1/4 Condiment)
- 1/4 cup light coconut milk, canned (1 Healthy Fat)
- 2 tsp. Thai fish sauce (2/3 Condiment)
- 1 tbsp. fresh basil, chopped (1/8 Condiment)

Directions:
Add shrimp in a hot skillet with 1 tbsp. oil and cook for 3 minutes. Add garlic powder, curry, and cook for 1 minute more. Then add the coconut milk and the fish sauce. Let simmer for 2 minutes and serve after sprinkling basil on top.

Servings: 1
Each serving provides 1 Leanest Lean, 2 Healthy Fats, and 3 Condiments

Swiss & Tuna

Ingredients:
- 2 Slices 2% reduced-fat Swiss Cheese Slices
- 8.8 oz. Tuna, drained

 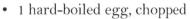 

- 1 hard-boiled egg, chopped
- 3 tbsp. light mayonnaise
- 1 tbsp. reduced-fat cream cheese
- 2 tsp. lemon juice
- 1/2 tsp. dried dill
- 1 oz. dill pickle relish
- 1/8 tsp. pepper
- 1/4 cup celery, chopped
- 2 Tomato Slices

Directions:
Combine all the ingredients except the tomato and the cheese slices in a mixing bowl. Prepare a baking tray with parchment paper and arrange the tomato slices on it. Divide the mixture over the slices and top with the cheese slices. Put it in the oven until the cheese is melted

Servings: 2
Each serving provides 3/4 Lean, 1/2 Green, 1 Healthy Fat, and 1.66 Condiments, 1/2 Fueling

Sweet Chili Shrimp

Ingredients:
- 9 oz. raw shrimp, peeled, tails removed (1 Leanest)
- 1/2 cup sweet red bell peppers (1 Green)
- 1/2 cup snap peas (1 Green)
- 2 tsp. sesame or olive oil (2 Healthy Fats)
- 1/2 cup riced cauliflower, cooked (1 Green)
- 1/2 tsp. sesame seeds (1/2 Condiment)

For the sauce:
- 2 tbsp. Sweet Chili Sauce (2 Condiments)
- 1/2 tbsp. soy sauce (1/2 Condiment)

Directions:
Preheat oven to 450°F. Mix together shrimps, peppers, sesame oil, and snap peas. Spread the mix on a baking tray with parchment paper. Bake for 10 minutes.

Prepare the sauce combining the ingredients above, drizzle it over the shrimps, and sprinkle sesame seeds all over
Servings: 1
Each serving provides 1 Leanest, 3 Greens, 3 Condiments and 2 Healthy Fats

Sushi Cone

Ingredients:
- 9 oz. raw shrimp (1 Leanest Lean)
- 2 Sheets Nori seaweed (2 Condiments)
- 1 1/4 cups cauliflower, cooked and grated (2 1/2 vegetable servings)
- 1/4 cup strips of cucumber (1/2 vegetable serving)
- 1/2 tbsp. lite soy sauce for marinade (1/2 Condiment)
- 1 tbsp. rice vinegar (1/4 Condiment)

Directions:
Marinate shrimps in soy sauce for at least 2 hours. Drain and cook the shrimps in a skillet. Assemble the sushi rolls by cutting the Nori sheet in half, placing it in your hand (shiny side down), spreading cauliflower on it, add fillings, and rolling the Nori sheet forming a cone shape.
Servings: 1
Each serving provides 1 Lean protein, 3 vegetable, and 2.75 Condiments

Marinara Shrimp Zoodles

Ingredients:
- 2 tsp. olive oil (2 Healthy Fats)
- 7 ounces thawed, cooked shrimp (1 Leanest Lean)
- 1 cup spiralized squash (2 Greens)
- 1/4 cup Marinara Sauce (1 Green)
- 1/4 tsp. Garlic Salt (1 Condiment)
- 1/2 tsp. Italian Seasonings (1 Condiment)
- 1 tbsp. Grated Parmesan Cheese (1 Condiment)

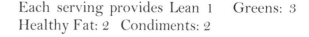

Directions:
Cook 4 minutes the squash in a skillet with oil over high heat. Add shrimps, sauce, garlic salt, and Italian seasoning. Cook 2 minutes, sprinkle with parmesan, and serve.

Servings: 1
Each serving provides 1 Leanest Lean, 3 Greens, 3 Condiments and 2 Healthy Fats

Lime & Garlic Shrimp

Ingredients:
- 21 oz. fully cooked frozen shrimp (3 Lean)
- 3 - 8 oz. packages angel hair noodles (6 Greens)
- 1 cup fresh tomatoes, diced (2 Greens)
- 1/2 cup green peppers, chopped (1 Green)
- 2 tbsp. olive oil (6 Healthy Fats)
- 1 tbsp. lime juice
- 1 clove garlic, minced

Seasoning blend:
- 1/4 tsp. salt
- 1/4 tsp. cayenne pepper
- 1/4 tsp. garlic powder
- 1/8 tsp. dried thyme
- 1/4 tsp. freshly ground black pepper
- 1/4 tsp. dried parsley flakes
- 1/4 tsp. paprika
- 1/8 tsp. onion powder

Directions:
Combine all the seasoning ingredients in a bowl to create a dry seasoning. In a hot large skillet put the oil and the garlic clove. Let cook for 1 minute and add the peppers, lime juice, and shrimps. Season with the entire bowl of the dry seasoning and cook for 5 minutes. Add in the drained noodles and cook 4 minutes more. Remove from heat and add the diced tomatoes.

Servings: 3

Each serving provides Lean 1   Greens: 3 Healthy Fat: 2   Condiments: 2

Scampi and Zucchini Ribbons

Ingredients:
- 9 oz. shrimp (1 Leanest Lean)
- 1 1/2 cup zucchini ribbons (3 Greens)
- 1 tbsp. light butter (1 Healthy Fat)
- 2 wedges light garlic and herb cheese (1 Healthy Fat)
- 1/4 cup low sodium chicken broth (1/4 Condiment)
- 1 clove garlic, minced (1 Condiment)
- 1 tsp. lemon (1/2 Condiment)
- 1/8 tsp. salt (1/2 Condiment)
- 1 tbsp. fresh Parsley (1/4 Condiment)
- 1 tsp. grated parmesan cheese (1/3 Condiment)

Directions:
Use a potato peeler to peel the zucchini until you reach the inner seeds. Take 1 ½ cup and save the residue for other recipes. Add garlic, butter, parsley, lemon juice, chicken broth, cheese, and salt in a large skillet over high heat. Once it boils reduce the heat and let simmer for 2 minutes. Add zucchini and cook 3 minutes more stirring frequently. Toss in the shrimps and turn the heat off. Sprinkle parmesan and serve.

Servings: 3
Each serving provides 1 Lean, 3 Greens, 3 Condiments and 2 Healthy Fats

Peanut Shrimp Salad

Ingredients:
- 1 1/2 cups shredded cabbage (3 Greens)
- 7 oz. cooked shrimp (1 Leanest)

Dressing:
- 2 tbsp. powdered peanut butter (1 Fueling)

- 1 1/2 tbsp. water
- 2 tsp. lite soy sauce (2/3 Condiment)
- 1/4 tsp. ground ginger (1/2 Condiment)
- 1/8 tsp. crushed red pepper (1/4 Condiment)
- 1/2 packet stevia (1/2 Condiment)
- 2 tsp. sesame oil (2 Healthy Fats)

Directions:
Combine shredded cabbage and shrimps in a bowl. Prepare the peanut dressing and pour over the shrimps and cabbage. Toss and serve!
Makes 1 Serving
Each serving provides 1 Leanest, 3 Greens, 2 Condiments, 2 Healthy Fats, and 1 Fueling

Shrimp & Cauliflower Fried Rice

Ingredients:
- 2 and 3/4 cup grated cauliflower (5 1/2 Greens)
- 1/4 cup green onion finely chopped (1/2 Green)
- 1/4 tsp. garlic powder (1/2 Condiment)
- 1/4 tsp. powdered ginger (1/2 Condiment)
- 3 tbsp. lite Soy Sauce (3 Condiments)
- 2 eggs, beaten (2/3 Lean)
- 9.3 oz. shrimp cooked (1 1/3 Lean)
- 2 tsp. sesame oil (2 Healthy Fats)

Directions:
Prepare scrambled eggs in a skillet sprayed with Pam. Let them moist. In another skillet heat the sesame oil and cook the chopped onion for 1 minute. Add in the cauliflower and cook 5 minutes more stirring constantly. Add the dry spices, the shrimps, the eggs, and the soy sauce. Cook 2 minutes more

Makes 1 Serving
Each serving provides 1 Lean, 3 Greens, 2 Condiments and 2 Healthy Fats

Shrimp and Cauliflower Grits

Preparation Time: 20 minutes
Cooking Time: 25 minutes
Servings: 4

Ingredients:
- 1-pound raw shrimps, peeled and deveined
- ½ tablespoon Cajun seasoning
- Cooking spray
- 1 tablespoon lemon juice
- ¼ cup chicken broth
- 1 tablespoon butter
- 2 ½ cups cauliflower, grated or minced finely
- ½ cup unsweetened cashew milk
- ¼ teaspoon salt
- 2 tablespoons sour cream
- 1/3 cup reduced-fat shredded cheddar cheese
- ¼ cup sliced scallions

Directions:
1) Place the shrimps and Cajun seasonings into a Ziploc bag and close the bag. Toss to coat the shrimps evenly with the seasoning.
2) Spray a skillet with cooking spray and cook the seasoned shrimps until pink. This will take about 2 to 3 minutes per side. Add the lemon juice and chicken broth. Make sure to scrape the bottom to remove the browned bits. Set aside.
3) In another skillet, heat butter over medium flame and add the rice cauliflower. Cook for 5 minutes and add the milk and salt. Cook for another 5 minutes. Remove from the heat and add the sour cream and cheese. Stir until well-combined.
4) Serve the shrimps on top of the cauliflower grits.
5) Garnish with scallions.

Nutrition: Calories: 456; 2 leanest protein, 3 healthy fat, 2 Greens. 1 Condiment.

Tuna Niçoise Salad

Preparation Time: 20 minutes
Cooking Time: 25 minutes
Servings: 4

Ingredients:
- 4 teaspoons extra virgin olive oil
- 3 tablespoons balsamic vinegar
- 2 garlic cloves (minced)
- 6 cups mixed greens
- 2 cups string beans (steamed)
- 1 cup cherry tomatoes (halved)
- 6 hard-boiled eggs (sliced)
- 2 7 ounces can of tuna, packed in water and drained

Directions:
1) Mix the oil, vinegar, and garlic in a bowl until well combined.
2) Place the remaining ingredients in a bowl and drizzle with the prepared sauce.

Nutrition: Calories: 392; 3 Greens, 1 healthy fat, 2 leanest protein.

Shrimp & Zucchini

Preparation Time: 20 minutes
Cooking Time: 30 minutes
Servings: 4

Ingredients:
- 1 lb. shrimp, peeled and deveined
- 1 zucchini (chopped)
- 1 summer squash (chopped)
- 2 tbsp. olive oil
- 1/2 small onion (chopped)
- 1/2 tsp. paprika
- 1/2 tsp. garlic powder
- 1/2 tsp. onion powder
- Pepper, Salt

Directions:
1) In a bowl, mix paprika, garlic powder, onion powder, pepper, and salt. Add shrimp and toss well.
2) Heat 1 tablespoon of oil in a pan over medium heat.
3) Add shrimp and cook for 2 minutes on each side or until shrimp turns to pink.
4) Transfer shrimp on a plate.
5) Add remaining oil in a pan.
6) Add onion, summer squash, and zucchini, then cook for 6-8 minutes or until vegetables are softened.
7) Return shrimp to the pan and cook for 1 minute.
8) Serve and enjoy.

Nutrition: Calories 215; 2 Green, 1 leanest protein, 1 Condiment.

Baked Dijon Salmon

Preparation Time: 20 minutes
Cooking Time: 50 minutes
Servings: 4

Ingredients:
- 1 1/2 lbs. salmon
- 1/4 cup Dijon mustard
- 1/4 cup fresh parsley (chopped)
- 1 tbsp. garlic (chopped)
- 1 tbsp. olive oil
- 1 tbsp. fresh lemon juice
- Pepper
- Salt

Directions:
1) Preheat the oven to 375°F. Line baking sheet with parchment paper.
2) Arrange salmon fillets on a prepared baking sheet.
3) In a small bowl, mix garlic, oil, lemon juice, Dijon mustard, parsley, pepper, and salt.
4) Brush salmon top with garlic mixture.

5) Bake for 18-20 minutes.
6) Serve and enjoy.

Nutrition: Calories 217; 3 servings healthy fat, 1 serving lean protein.

VEGETABLES

Cauliflower Pizza Crust

Ingredients:
- 1 cup shredded cauliflower (2 Greens)
- 1 oz. low-fat ricotta with (1/8 Lean)
- 1 oz. light Mozzarella (2/8 Lean)
- 1/4 cup Egg Beaters (1/8 Lean)
- 1/8 tsp. garlic powder (1/4 Condiment)
- 1/4 tsp. dried basil (1/8 Condiment)

Toppings:
- 2 oz. light cheese blend (1/2 lean)
- 1/4 cup marinara sauce (1 Green)

Directions:
Mix together all the ingredients until well combined. Prepare a baking tray with parchment paper and spray it with cooking spray. Create a pizza crust in the tray and cook at 400°F for 30 minutes. Then flip them and cook 20 minutes more. Adjust cooking time to the thickness of the pizza crust. Top with tomato and cheese, then put it back in the oven for 10 minutes more.
Serving 1

 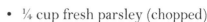

Each serving is 1 Complete Lean and Green Meal with less than 1 Condiment

Chipotle Mac and Cheese Waffles

Preparation Time: 20 minutes
Cooking Time: 35 minutes
Servings: 4

Ingredients:
- 2 sachets Branded Select Chipotle Mac and Cheese
- 4 ounces cold water
- 6 tablespoons liquid egg whites
- Cooking spray
- 1 teaspoon hot sauce
- 2 tablespoon sugar-free maple syrup

Directions:
1) In a medium-sized microwave-safe bowl, mix the Chipotle Mac and Cheese with water. Mix until well combined.
2) Microwave on high heat for 1 ½ minute. Let it stand for 1 minute. Repeat three times. Allow to cool and whisk in the liquid egg whites.
3) Pour the mixture into a greased waffle iron. Close the lid and bake for 5 minutes until cooked. Remove from the waffle iron and serve with hot sauce and maple syrup.

Nutrition: Calories: 242; 1 Fueling, 3 Condiments.

Cucumber Bowl with Spices and Greek Yogurt

Preparation Time: 10 minutes
Cooking Time: 20 minutes
Servings: 3

Ingredients:
- 4 cucumbers
- ½ teaspoon chili pepper
- ¼ cup fresh parsley (chopped)
- ¾ cup fresh dill (chopped)
- 2 tablespoons lemon juice
- ½ teaspoon salt
- ½ teaspoon ground black pepper
- ¼ teaspoon sage
- ½ teaspoon dried oregano
- 1/3 cup Greek yogurt

Directions:
1) Make the cucumber dressing: blend the dill and parsley until you get a green mash.
2) Then combine the green mash with lemon juice, salt, ground black pepper, sage, dried oregano, Greek yogurt, and chili pepper.
3) Churn the mixture well.
4) Chop the cucumbers roughly and combine them with cucumber dressing. Mix up well.
5) Refrigerate the cucumber for 20 minutes.

Nutrition: Calories: 114 Carbs: 3 Greens, 1 leaner protein.

Stuffed Bell Peppers with Quinoa

Preparation Time: 10 minutes
Cooking Time: 35 minutes
Servings: 2

Ingredients:
- 2 bell peppers
- 1/3 cup quinoa
- 3 oz. chicken stock
- ¼ cup onion (diced)
- ½ teaspoon salt
- ¼ teaspoon tomato paste
- ½ teaspoon dried oregano
- 1/3 cup sour cream
- 1 teaspoon paprika

Directions:

1) Trim the peppers and remove the seeds
2) Then combine chicken stock and quinoa in the pan.
3) Add salt and boil the ingredients for 10 minutes or until quinoa soaks all liquid.
4) Then combine the cooked quinoa with dried oregano, tomato paste, and onion.
5) Fill the bell peppers with the quinoa mixture and arrange in the casserole mold.
6) Add sour cream and bake the peppers for 25 minutes at 365° F.
7) Serve the cooked peppers with sour cream sauce from the casserole mold.

Nutrition: Calories: 237; 2 Greens, 1 healthy fat.

Spaghetti Squash Gratin

Preparation Time: 10 minutes
Cooking Time: 60 minutes
Servings: 2

Ingredients:
- 2 ½ pounds spaghetti squash
- 2 eggs
- 1 cup reduced-fat cheddar cheese (shredded)
- ½ cup plain low-fat Greek yogurt
- 2 cloves garlic (minced)
- Salt and pepper to taste
- ½ cup reduced-fat grated parmesan cheese

Directions:
1) Preheat the oven to 400° F.
2) Halve the spaghetti squash and scoop out the seeds. Put squash face down on a baking sheet lined with foil. Place in the oven and cook for 30 minutes. Allow cooling before scooping the meat and placing in a large bowl.
3) In another bowl, combine the remaining ingredients. Mix well until well combined.

4) Spread in a casserole dish and bake for 30 more minutes in the oven.

Nutrition: Calories: 503; 2 Greens, 1 leanest protein, 1 leaner protein.

Mex Mac and Cheese

Ingredients:
- 7.5 oz. cooked 93% lean ground beef, fat drained (1 1/2 Leans)
- 2 tsp. low sodium taco seasoning mix (4 Condiments)
- 5 cups cooked cauliflower, cut into small florets (10 Greens)
- 1/2 cup chopped green chilies (1 Green)
- 1/2 cup green or red peppers, diced (1 Green)
- 1 oz. pickled jalapenos, chopped (1 Fueling)

For the sauce:
- 1 cup unsweetened cashew milk (1 Condiment)
- 4 tbsp. reduced-fat cream cheese (4 Condiments)
- 1 tsp. Dijon mustard (1 Condiment)
- 1 tbsp. reduced-fat grated parmesan cheese (1/2 Condiment)
- 1/4 tsp. garlic powder (1/2 Condiment)
- 1 1/2 cups sharp cheddar cheese (1 1/2 Leans)

Topping:
- 1 cup shredded reduced-fat Mexican cheese (1 Lean)

Directions:
Preheat oven to 375 °F. Spray a 9x9 casserole with Pam. Mix the ground beef with the taco seasoning and cook in a skillet over medium heat for 4 minutes. Remove from heat and add cauliflower, peppers, and jalapenos. Prepare the sauce mixing the ingredients in a saucepan over medium-low

heat until sauce is smooth. Pour the cheese sauce into the meat-cauliflower casserole and mix. Sprinkle the cheese topping on it and bake for 15 minutes before serving.

Serving 4
Each serving is 1 Lean, 3 Greens, 2.75 Condiments and 1/4 Fueling

Cauliflower Mac and Cheese

Ingredients:
- 3 cups Cauliflower –Steamed and chopped (6 Greens)
- 2 cup reduced-fat shredded Cheddar (2 Lean)
- 2 Tbsp. reduced-fat cream cheese (2 Condiments)
- 1/8 tsp. salt (1/2 Condiment)
- 1/4 tsp. garlic powder (1/2 Condiment)
- 1/4 tsp. onion powder (1/2 Condiment)
- 1/4 tsp. ground mustard (1/2 Condiment)

Directions:
Preheat oven to 350°F. Prepare a saucepan over very low heat with cream cheese, salt, garlic powder, onion powder, and mustard. Whisk until smooth, then add the cheese and stir until it melts completely. Finally, add the cauliflower and stir gently to cover them. Place the mix in a baking dish and bake for 20 minutes.

Serving 2
Each serving is 1 Lean, 3 Greens, and 2 Condiments

Cauliflower Mac and Cheese - 2

Ingredients:
- 1 1/2 cups chopped cauliflower, cooked (3 Greens)
- 1/2 cup 1% cottage cheese (1/3 Lean)
- 2.6 oz. 2% reduced-fat cheddar cheese, shredded (2/3 Lean)

- 1/4 tsp. ground mustard (1/2 condiment)
- 1/4 tsp. garlic powder (1 condiment)
- 1/4 tsp. onion powder (1/2 condiment)
- 1/8 tsp. salt (1/2 condiment)

Directions:
Preheat oven to 350°F. Blend all the ingredients, except cauliflower. Pour the mixture over cauliflower and stir. Pour into a casserole dish sprayed with Pam. Bake for 35 minutes.

Serving 1
Each serving is 1 complete lean and green with 2 1/2 condiments

Spaghetti Squash Teriyaki

Ingredients:
- 1 cup spaghetti squash, cooked (2 Greens)
- 1/2 cup shredded cabbage (1 Green)
- 1 tsp. sesame oil (1 Healthy Fat)
- 1 clove garlic, minced (1 Condiment)
- 2 tsp. lite soy sauce (2/3 Condiment)
- 1 tsp. teriyaki sauce (1 Condiment)

Directions:
Heat the oil and garlic in a skillet. Once the garlic is brown, add the spaghetti squash and the cabbage. Cook one minute and add the sauces. Cook 5 minutes more.

Serving 1
Each serving is 3 Greens, 1 Healthy Fat, and 2.6 Condiments

Zucchini and Tomato Skillet

Ingredients:
- 1 clove garlic, minced (1 Condiment)
- 1 tsp. olive oil (1 Healthy Fat)
- 1/2 packet stevia - optional (1/2 Condiment)
- 1/2 teaspoon salt (2 Condiments)
- 1/2 tsp. dried basil (1/2 Condiment)

- 1 1/2 tsp. grated reduced-fat grated parmesan cheese, divided (1/2 Condiment)
- 3 cups zucchini, sliced 1/2-inch thick (6 greens)
- 1 1/2 cups tomatoes, diced (3 Greens)

Directions:
Heat the oil and garlic in a skillet. Once the garlic is brown, add sugar, salt, pepper, basil, and zucchini. Cook for 5 minutes and add tomatoes. Cook for 2 minutes more and divide into servings. Sprinkle parmesan on top.
Serving 1
Each serving provides 1 ½ Greens, 1.16 Condiments and 1/3 Healthy Fat

Turnip Fries

Ingredients:
- 1 1/2 cups turnips, sliced into steak fries (3 Greens)
- 1 tsp. olive oil (1 healthy fat)
- Sea salt, pepper, and garlic powder to taste

Directions:
Preheat oven to 425 °F. Combine all the ingredients and spread on a baking tray. Bake for 30 minutes.

Serving 1
Each serving is 3 Greens and 1 Healthy Fat

Jicama Fries

Ingredients:
- 3 cups jicama, sliced (6 Greens)
- 2 tsp. olive oil (2 Healthy Fats)
- 1/2 tsp. paprika (1 Condiment)
- 1/4 tsp. onion powder (1/2 Condiment)
- 1/4 tsp. garlic powder (1/2 Condiment)
- salt and pepper, if desired

Directions:

Preheat oven to 425 °F. Remove skin and top off the jicama, then cut it in sticks. Boil the sticks for 10 minutes and after that completely drain them. Be sure to remove all the water from the outside. Mix them with the other ingredients and spread them on a baking tray. Bake 45 minutes, flipping them halfway.

Serving 1
Each serving 3 Greens, 1 Condiment, and 1 Healthy Fats

Jicama Tuna Salad Stuffed Peppers

Ingredients:
- 4.6 oz. drained canned tuna (2/3 Lean)
- 1 1/2 Tbsp. lite mayo (1 Healthy Fat)
- 1/4 tsp. seasoning of choice (1 Condiment)
- 1 tsp. Dijon mustard (1 Condiment)
- 1 tsp. lime juice (1/2 Condiment)
- 1/8 tsp. fresh ground black pepper (1/4 Condiment)
- 2 tbsp. fresh cilantro, finely chopped (1/8 Condiment)
- 1/4 cup celery, chopped (1/2 Green)
- 1/4 cup jicama, chopped (1/2 Green)
- 1 bell pepper sliced in half lengthwise, top and membrane removed (2 Greens)
- 2 slices Reduced-fat cheddar cheese slices (1/3 Lean)

Directions:
Shred tuna with a fork. Combine it with the other ingredients except for the peppers and the cheddar slices. Stuff the peppers with the mix and place the cheddar slices on top of each half pepper. Bake them at 400°F for 2 minutes.

Serving 1
Each serving provides 1 Lean, 3 Greens, 3 Condiments, and 1 Healthy Fat

Broccoli Chicken Dijon

Ingredients:
- 1 lb. boneless skinless chicken breasts, cut in thin strips (2 Leaner)
- ¼ cup reduced-sodium chicken broth (¼ Condiment)
- 1 ½ tbsp. light soy sauce (1 ½ Condiment)
- 3 cups broccoli florets (6 Greens)
- 1 clove garlic, minced (1 Condiment)
- 2 teaspoons olive oil (2 Healthy Fats)
- 1 tbsp. Dijon mustard (3 Condiments)

Directions:
Marinade the chicken strips with soy sauce for at least 1 hour. Heat 1 tbsp. olive oil and garlic in a skillet. Once the garlic is brown, add broccoli and cook for five minutes stirring frequently. In another skillet, cook the drained chicken strips with the remaining oil for 5 minutes. Add chicken broth, the mustard and bring to a boil. Once it thickens, add the broccoli and remove it from heat. Stir and serve

Serving 2
Each serving provides 1 Lean, 3 Greens, 3 Condiments, and 1 Healthy Fat

Hamburger Cabbage Stir Fry

Ingredients:
- 16 oz. raw 95 to 97% lean ground beef (2 Leaner)
- 2 tsp. sesame oil (2 Healthy Fats)
- 2 1/2 cups cabbage, shredded (5 Greens)
- 1/2 cup any color bell pepper, chopped (1 Green)
- 2 tbsp. lite soy sauce (2 Condiments)
- 1/2 tsp. garlic powder (1 Condiment)
- 1/2 tsp. ground ginger (1 Condiment)
- 1/2 packet Stevia (1/2 Condiment)
- 1/4 tsp. salt (1 Condiment)
- 1/4 tsp. black pepper (1/2 Condiment)

Directions:
Heat the oil in a skillet and cook the beef for 5 minutes, stirring frequently. Add the other ingredients and stir-fry for 7 minutes.

Serving 2
Each serving provides 1 Lean, 3 Green, 3 Condiments, and 1 Healthy Fats

Cajun Style Shrimp Skillet

Ingredients:
- 1 tbsp. light butter (1 Healthy Fat)
- 1 tbsp. olive oil (3 Healthy Fats)
- 1 tsp. minced garlic (1 Condiment)
- 18 oz. raw shrimp, cleaned (2 Leanest Leans)
- 1 1/4 tsp. Cajun seasoning (5 Condiments)
- 1/2 cup assorted bell peppers, chopped (1 Green)
- 1/2 cup Great Value Italian diced tomatoes, canned (1 Green)
- 2 cups frozen cauliflower rice (4 Greens)

Directions:
Heat the oil, garlic, and butter in a skillet. Add shrimps and sprinkle Cajun seasoning. Cook for 4 minutes and add the vegetables. Cook 4 minutes more and serve

Serving 2
Each serving provides 1 Leanest, 3 Greens, 3 Condiments and 2 Healthy Fats

Cauliflower Bread

Ingredients:
- 1 cup raw grated cauliflower (2 Greens)
- 1/4 cup liquid egg substitute (1.3 Condiments)
- 1/8 tsp. Garlic salt (1/2 Condiment)
- 1/4 tsp. dried Basil (1/8 Condiment)
- 1/4 tsp. dried Oregano (1/4 Condiment)
- 1/4 cup Marinara Sauce (1 Green)

Directions:

Preheat oven to 350°F. Mix all the ingredients in a bowl, except the marinara sauce. Pour the mixture in a 9" by 5" loaf pan with parchment paper and create a loaf 1 inch thick. Bake for 30 minutes, flip it, and bake 15 minutes more at 450°F.

Serving 2
Each serving provides 1 Lean, 2.25 Condiments and 3 Greens

Curry Roasted Cauliflower

Ingredients:
- 4 1/2 cups raw cauliflower cut into florets (9 Greens)
- 1 tbsp. olive oil (3 Healthy Fats)
- 1 tsp. curry powder (2 Condiments)
- 1/2 tsp. smoked paprika (1 Condiment)
- 1/2 tsp. garlic salt (2 Condiments)

Directions:

Preheat oven to 425 °F. Mix in a bowl oil and cauliflower florets, then put the spices, the garlic salt, and stir to combine. Bake in a baking tray with parchment paper for 25 minutes stirring halfway.

Serving 3
Each serving provides 3 Greens, 1.7 Condiments, and 1 Healthy Fat

Cauliflower Salad

Ingredients:
- 1 1/2 cups cauliflower, cooked and chopped into small bites (3 Greens)
- 2 cooked hard-boiled eggs (2/3 Lean)
- 1/2 cup 2% plain Greek yogurt (1/3 Lean)
- 2 tsp. Dijon mustard (2 Condiments)
- 1/8 tsp. salt (1/2 Condiment)
- 1/8 tsp. fresh black pepper (1/4 Condiment)
- 1/8 tsp. paprika (1/4 Condiment)
- 2 pickle spears, chopped (1 Snack)

Directions:

Place cauliflower in a medium-sized bowl with chopped boiled eggs and pickles. Add yogurt, Dijon mustard, salt, pepper and paprika. Mix until well combined, and refrigerate before serving.

Serving 3
Each serving provides 1 Lean, 3 Greens, 3 Condiments and 1 Fueling.

Veggie Dips and Buffalo Dip

Preparation Time: 20 minutes
Cooking Time: 25 minutes
Servings: 4

Ingredients:
- 1 tablespoon olive oil
- 2 teaspoons lemon juice
- ½ teaspoon salt
- ½ teaspoon pepper
- ½ teaspoon rosemary
- 4 cups sliced yellow squash
- 3 cups sliced zucchini
- 4 light spreadable cheese wedges
- 1 ½ cup plain low-fat Greek yoghurt
- ¼ cup light ranch dressing

Directions:
1) Preheat the oven to 400°F.
2) In a bowl, put the oil, lemon juice, salt, pepper, rosemary, and vegetables. Toss to coat the vegetables.
3) Arrange the vegetables in a baking sheet in a single layer.
4) Bake for 20 minutes until crisp.
5) Meanwhile, place the remaining ingredients in a bowl. Whisk to combine the dip.
6) Serve the crispy vegetables with the dip.

Nutrition: Calories: 140; 3 Greens, 1 healthy fat serving, 1 serving lean protein.

Grilled Tempeh with Eggplants and Watercress

Preparation Time: 20 minutes
Cooking Time: 35 minutes
Servings: 4

Ingredients:
- 20 ounces tempeh, sliced into large chunks
- 4 ½ cups diced eggplants
- ½ tablespoons rice vinegar
- ½ teaspoon ground black pepper
- ½ teaspoon salt (divided)
- 1 ½ cups watercress
- ¼ cup minced scallions
- ½ cup fresh tomatoes (sliced)
- ½ tablespoon lemon juice
- 1 ½ tablespoon soy sauce
- 1 teaspoon lime juice

Directions:
1) Pour boiling water over the tempeh and allow it to soak for 30 minutes.
2) In a bowl, toss the eggplant together with the rice vinegar, pepper, and a quarter of the salt.
3) Fire the grill to 425°F and roast the seasoned eggplants for 30 minutes on all sides until golden brown and tender.
4) Remove the roasted eggplants and allow it to cool.
5) Pat-dry the tempeh and grill for 2 minutes on each side until golden brown. Set aside to cool.
6) Prepare the watercress salad by combining the remaining ingredients in a bowl. Toss to coat.
7) Serve the tempeh, grilled eggplants, and watercress together.

Nutrition: Calories: 310; 1 Lean; 3 greens; 2 Condiments.

Easy Spinach Muffins

Preparation Time: 20 minutes

Cooking Time: 25 minutes
Servings: 4

Ingredients:
- 10 eggs
- 2 cups spinach (chopped)
- 1/4 tsp. garlic powder
- 1/4 tsp. onion powder
- 1/2 tsp. dried basil
- 1 1/2 cups parmesan cheese (grated)
- Salt

Directions:
1) Preheat the oven to 400 0 F. Grease muffin tin and set aside.
2) In a large bowl, whisk eggs with basil, garlic powder, onion powder, and salt.
3) Add cheese and spinach and stir well.
4) Pour egg mixture into the prepared muffin tin and bake 15 minutes.
5) Serve and enjoy.

Nutrition: Calories 110; 1 lean protein, 1 healthy fat.

Cauliflower Spinach Rice

Preparation Time: 20 minutes
Cooking Time: 30 minutes
Servings: 4

Ingredients:
- 5 oz. baby spinach
- 4 cups cauliflower rice
- 1 tsp. garlic (minced)
- 3 tbsp. olive oil
- 1 fresh lime juice
- 1/4 cup vegetable broth
- 1/4 tsp. chili powder
- Pepper
- Salt

Directions:
1) Heat olive oil in a pan over medium heat.

2) Add garlic and sauté for 30 seconds. Add cauliflower rice, chili powder, pepper, and salt then cook for 2 minutes.
3) Add broth and lime juice and stir well.
4) Add spinach and stir until spinach is wilted.
5) Serve and enjoy.

Nutrition: Calories 147; 3 Greens, 1 healthy fat.

Tofu Scramble

Preparation Time: 20 minutes
Cooking Time: 30 minutes
Servings: 4

Ingredients:
- 1/2 block firm tofu (crumbled)
- 1 cup spinach
- 1/4 cup zucchini (chopped)
- 1 tbsp. olive oil
- 1 tomato (chopped)
- 1/4 tsp. ground cumin
- 1 tbsp. turmeric
- 1 tbsp. coriander (chopped)
- 1 tbsp. chives (chopped)
- Pepper, Salt

Directions:
1) Heat the oil in a pan over medium heat.
2) Add tomato, zucchini, and spinach and sauté for 2 minutes.
3) Add tofu, turmeric, cumin, pepper, and salt, and sauté for 5 minutes.
4) Garnish with chives and coriander.
5) Serve and enjoy.

Nutrition: Calories 102; 3 Greens, 1 healthy fat, 1 lean protein.

Grilled Tofu and Zucchini

Preparation Time: 20 minutes
Cooking Time: 30 minutes

Servings: 4

Ingredients:
- 3 ½ pounds firm tofu (sliced)
- 2 teaspoons extra virgin olive oil (divided)
- 1 teaspoon crushed garlic
- 2 teaspoons balsamic vinegar
- 1 zucchini (sliced to ¼ inch thick)
- Salt and pepper to taste

Directions:
1) Preheat the grill to 425° F
2) Place all ingredients in a bowl and toss to coat both tofu slices and zucchini with the seasoning.
3) Place the zucchini and tofu on the grill and cook for 5 minutes on each side.
4) Serve immediately.

Nutrition: Calories: 395; 2 servings healthy fat, 1 serving lean protein, 1 serving higher carb.

Healthy Cauliflower Grits

Preparation Time: 20 minutes
Cooking Time: 30 minutes
Servings: 4

Ingredients:
- 6 cups cauliflower rice
- 1/4 tsp. garlic powder
- 1 cup cream cheese
- 1/2 cup vegetable stock
- 1/4 tsp. onion powder
- 1/2 tsp. pepper
- 1 tsp. Salt

Directions:
1) Add all ingredients into the slow cooker and stir well to combine.
2) Cover and cook on low for 2 hours.
3) Stir and serve.

Nutrition: Calories 126; 2 Greens, 1 serving healthy fat.

Cauliflower Broccoli Mash

Preparation Time: 20 minutes
Cooking Time: 30 minutes
Servings: 4

Ingredients:
- 1 lb. cauliflower, cut into florets
- 2 cups broccoli (chopped)
- 1 tsp. garlic (minced)
- 1 tsp. dried rosemary
- 1/4 cup olive oil
- Salt

Directions:
1) Add broccoli and cauliflower into the instant pot.
2) Pour enough water into the instant pot to cover broccoli and cauliflower.
3) Seal the pot and cook on high pressure for 12 minutes.

4) Once done, allow to release pressure naturally. Remove lid.
5) Drain broccoli and cauliflower and clean the instant pot.
6) Add oil into the instant pot and set the pot on sauté mode.
7) Add broccoli, cauliflower, rosemary, garlic, and salt then cook for 10 minutes.
8) Mash the broccoli and cauliflower mixture using a masher until smooth.

Nutrition: Calories 205; 3 Greens, 1 Healthy Fat.

Zucchini and Tomato Skillet

Preparation Time: 20 minutes
Cooking Time: 30 minutes
Servings: 4

Ingredients:
- 1 teaspoon olive oil
- 1 clove garlic (minced)
- 1 ½ cups tomatoes (peeled and diced)
- ½ teaspoon salt
- ½ teaspoon dried basil
- A dash of pepper
- 3 cups zucchini slices
- 1 ½ teaspoon grated fat-reduced parmesan cheese

Directions:
1) Heat oil in a skillet over medium flame and sauté the garlic for 30 seconds or until fragrant. Add in the tomatoes and stir for 1 minute.
2) Add in salt, basil, pepper, and zucchini slices.
3) Lower the heat to medium-low and stir for another 5 minutes.
4) Turn off the heat and garnish with parmesan cheese before serving.

Nutrition: Calories: 91; 2 Green, 1 servings healthy fat, 1 Condiment

SALADS

Avocado Chicken Salad

Ingredients:
- 10 oz. finely diced chicken, about 2 cups but weigh for accuracy (1 2/3 Lean)
- 1/2 cup 2% Plain Greek yogurt (1/3 Lean)
- 3 oz. chopped avocado (2 Healthy Fats)
- 1/2 tsp. garlic powder (1 Condiment)
- 1/4 tsp. salt (1 Condiment)
- 1/8 tsp. pepper (1/2 Condiment)
- 1 tbsp. + 1 tsp. lime juice (2 Condiments)
- 1/4 cup fresh cilantro, chopped (1/4 Condiment)

Directions:
Combine all the ingredients in a bowl. Refrigerate before serve

Servings: 2
Each serving provides 1 Lean, 2.3 Condiments, and 1 Healthy Fat

Super Rolls

Ingredients:
- 3 eggs at room temp (1 Lean)
- 3 tbsp. light cream cheese at room temperature (3 Condiments)
- A pinch or 1/16 tsp. cream of tartar (you can use white vinegar or lemon juice as a substitute)
- 1 packet stevia (1 Condiment)

Directions:
Preheat oven to 350°F. Separate egg whites from yolks, putting them in 2 different bowls. Add cream of tartar to egg whites. Beat egg whites on high until stiff peaks form. Set aside. Add cream cheese and stevia to yolks. Whisk until blended. Gently whisk the yolk mixture into egg whites. Be careful to wish from the downside up to avoid egg whites falling. On a cookie sheet lined with parchment paper, make six equal-sized blobs, not touching. Bake for 30 minutes.

Servings: 3 – 2 rolls each
Each serving provides 1/3 Lean and 1.3 Condiments

Burger Salad

Ingredients:
- 2 1/2 cups lettuce, shredded (2 1/2 Greens)
- 1/4 cup tomatoes, chopped (1/2 Green)
- 4.5 ounces lean 95 - 97% ground beef, cooked (3/4 Lean)
- 1/4 cup reduced-fat shredded cheddar cheese (1/4 Lean)
- 2 dill pickle spears, chopped (1 Fueling)
- 1 tbsp. onion, chopped (1 Condiment)
- 1/2 tsp. sesame seeds (1/2 Condiment)

Dressing:
- 2 tbsp. Wish-bone Lite dressing (1 Healthy Fat)
- 1/8 tsp. white wine vinegar
- 1/8 tsp. onion powder (1/4 Condiment)

Directions:
Combine all the dressing ingredients in a bowl and set it aside. Combine lettuce, tomatoes, ground beef, cheese, pickles, and onion in a medium-sized bowl. Top with dressing and sesame seeds. Enjoy!

Servings: 1
Each serving provides 1 Lean, 3 Greens, 1.75 Condiments, 1 Healthy Fat, and 1 Fueling.

Caprese Salad

Ingredients:
- 4 oz. fresh mozzarella between 3 to 6 g fat per oz., cubed (1 Lean)
- 1 cup baby spinach (1 Green)
- 1 cup Roma or heirloom tomatoes, sliced (2 Greens)
- 1/4 cup fresh chopped basil (1/4 Condiment)

- 1/8 tsp. salt (1/2 Condiment)
- 1/8 tsp. pepper (1/4 Condiment)
- 2 tbsp. Balsamic Vinaigrette Dressing (1 Condiment)

Directions:
On a plate layer spinach and then tomatoes. Season with salt and pepper. Add mozzarella on top. Drizzle dressing on top of the mozzarella and then top with fresh basil. Enjoy!

Servings: 1
Each serving provides 1 Lean, 3 Greens, and 2 Condiments

Coleslaw

Ingredients:
- 1 1/2 cups coleslaw mix - take out the carrots (3 Greens)
- 2 tsp. apple cider vinegar (1/6 Condiment)
- 1 tsp. olive oil (1 Healthy Fat)
- 1/2 packet of stevia, or to taste (1/2 Condiment)

Directions:
Combine all ingredients in a bowl. Enjoy!

Servings: 1
Each serving provides 3 Greens, less than 1 Condiment, and 1 Healthy Fat.

Cauliflower Salad

Ingredients:
- 1 1/2 cups cauliflower, cooked from frozen (3 Greens)
- 2 cooked hard-boiled eggs chopped (2/3 Lean)
- 1/2 cup 2% plain Greek yogurt (1/3 Lean)
- 2 tsp. Dijon mustard (2 Condiments)
- 1/8 tsp. salt (1/2 Condiment)

- 1/8 tsp. fresh black pepper (1/4 Condiment)
- 1/8 tsp. paprika (1/4 Condiment)
- 2 pickle spears, chopped (1 Snack)

Directions:
Chop cooked cauliflower into small florets and place them in a bowl. Add eggs and pickles. In another small bowl, combine yogurt, Dijon mustard, salt, pepper, and paprika. Add to the cauliflower mix and toss. Serve refrigerated.

Servings: 1
Each serving provides 1 Lean, 3 Greens, 3 Condiments and 1 Fueling.

Jalapeno Chicken Salad

Ingredients:
- 20 oz. cooked chicken breasts, diced (4 Leaner with 8 slices of turkey bacon)
- 1/4 cup chopped red onion ~ optional (4 Condiments)
- 1/2 cup 2% plain Greek yogurt (1/3 Leaner)
- 2.5 ounces (about 1/4 cup) pickled jalapenos, chopped (2 1/2 Fuelings)
- 1 tbsp. juice from jarred jalapenos
- 8 tbsp. light cream cheese, softened (8 Condiments)
- 1/4 cup plus 2 tbsp. light mayonnaise (4 Healthy Fats)
- 1/4 tsp. garlic salt (1 Condiment)
- 8 slices turkey bacon, cooked and chopped (4 ounces of protein)
- 2/3 cup reduced-fat sharp cheddar cheese (2/3 Lean)

Directions:
Combine all the ingredients except the turkey bacon in a large bowl and stir until combined. Gently stir in turkey bacon and cheddar cheese. Divide into 5 equal portions and serve as a lettuce wrap.

Servings: 5
Each serving provides 1 Leaner, 1 Condiments, 1 Healthy Fat, and 1/2 Fueling

Egg Salad

Ingredients:
- 6 Hard-boiled Eggs, peeled and chopped (2 Leans)
- 2 tsp. Dijon mustard (2 Condiments)
- 4 tbsp. low fat plain Greek yogurt (2 Condiments)
- 2 tbsp. fresh chives, finely chopped (1/2 Condiment)
- 1/4 tsp. salt (1 Condiment)
- 1/4 tsp. paprika (1/2 Condiment)
- 2 dill pickle spear, finely chopped* (1 Fueling)

Directions:
Combine all the ingredients in a bowl and gently stir until combined. Refrigerate leftovers in an airtight container for up to 3 days.

Servings: 1
Each serving provides 1 Lean, 3 Condiments, and 1/2 Fueling

Peanut Shrimp Salad

Ingredients:
- 1 1/2 cups tri-color coleslaw mix (3 Greens)
- 7 oz. cooked shrimp - (1 Leanest)
Dressing:
- 2 tbsp. powdered peanut butter (1 Fueling)
- 1 1/2 tbsp. water
- 2 tsp. lite soy sauce (2/3 Condiment)
- 1/4 tsp. ground ginger (1/2 Condiment)
- 1/8 tsp. crushed red pepper (1/4 Condiment)
- 1/2 packet stevia or to taste (1/2 Condiment)

 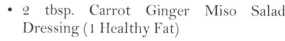

- 2 tsp. sesame oil (2 Healthy Fats)

Directions:
Combine coleslaw mix and shrimp in a bowl. Mix all the ingredients for the peanut dressing together in a small bowl and Pour it over shrimp and veggies.

Servings: 1
Each serving provides 1 Leanest, 3 Greens, 2 Condiments, 2 Healthy Fats, and 1 Fueling

Taco Salad

Ingredients:
- 6.5 oz. of 95 to 97% lean ground beef (3/4 Leaner Lean)
- 1 1/2 tsp. low sodium taco seasoning mix (3 Condiments)
- 2 tbsp. water
- 2 cups lettuce, chopped (2 Green)
- 1/2 cup tomatoes, chopped (1 Green)
- 1 oz. or 1/4 cup 2% reduced-fat Mexican Cheese (1/4 Lean)
- 2 tbsp. Hidden Valley Light Ranch Dressing (1 Healthy Fat)

Directions:
Cook ground turkey in a skillet. Drain the fat and them again in the pan. Stir in the water and taco seasoning mix. Simmer for about 5 minutes. Serve meat over lettuce and tomatoes. Sprinkle with cheese and add the salad dressing.

Servings: 1
Each serving provides 1 Lean, 3 Greens, 3 Condiments, and 1 Healthy Fat

Shrimp Burger Salad

Ingredients:
- 2 Shrimp Burgers (1 Leaner)
- 3 cups Baby Spring Mix (3 Greens)

- 2 tbsp. Carrot Ginger Miso Salad Dressing (1 Healthy Fat)

Directions:
Cook shrimp burgers on a non-stick skillet sprayed with cooking spray over medium-high heat for 4 to 5 minutes on each side. Add spring mix to a large bowl. Top with shrimp burgers and drizzle with dressing. Enjoy!

Servings: 1
Each serving provides 1 Leaner, 3 Greens, and 1 Healthy Fat

Healthy Broccoli Salad

Preparation Time: 20 minutes
Cooking Time: 10 minutes
Servings: 4

Ingredients:
- 3 cups broccoli (chopped)
- 1 tbsp. apple cider vinegar
- ½ cup Greek yogurt
- 2 tbsp. sunflower seeds
- 3 bacon slices (cooked and chopped)
- 1/3 cup onion (sliced)
- ¼ tsp. stevia

Directions:
1) In a mixing bowl, mix broccoli, onion, and bacon.
2) In a small bowl, mix yogurt, vinegar, and stevia and pour over broccoli mixture. Stir to combine.
3) Sprinkle sunflower seeds on top of the salad.
4) Store the salad in the refrigerator for 30 minutes.
5) Serve and enjoy.

Nutrition: Calories 90; 1 serving healthy fat, 1 serving higher carb. I serving lean protein, 1 serving leaner protein.

SOUPS

Bacon Cheeseburger Soup

Ingredients:
- 2.5 oz. 93% lean ground beef, cooked (1/2 Lean)
- 1 oz. 2% reduced-fat Mexican Cheese
- 2 slices turkey bacon, cooked and crumbled (1/2 Lean with the cheese)
- 1 cup low sodium beef broth (1 Condiment)
- 1 wedge Light Garlic and Herb Laughing Cow Cheese (1 Condiment)
- 1/2 cup Italian diced tomatoes in juice (1 Green)

Directions:

Combine all ingredients in a saucepan and cook over medium high heat until cheese has melted.

Servings: 1
Each serving provides 1 Lean, 1 Green, and 2 Condiments

Cheeseburger Soup

Preparation Time: 20 minutes
Cooking Time: 25 minutes
Servings: 4

Ingredients:
- ¼ cup of chopped onion

- 1 quantity of 14.5 oz. can have diced tomato
- 1 lb. of 90% lean ground beef
- ¾ cup of diced celery
- 2 teaspoon of Worcestershire sauce
- 3 cups of low sodium chicken broth
- ¼ teaspoon of salt
- 1 teaspoon of dried parsley
- 7 cups of baby spinach
- ¼ teaspoon of ground pepper
- 4 oz. of reduced-fat shredded cheddar cheese

Directions:
1) Get a large soup pot and cook the beef until it becomes brown. Add the celery, onion, and sauté until it becomes tender. Remove from the fire and drain excess liquid.
2) Stir in the broth, tomatoes, parsley, Worcestershire sauce, pepper, and salt. Cover and allow it to simmer on low heat for about 20 minutes
3) Add spinach and leave it to cook until it becomes wilted in about 1-3 minutes. Top each of your servings with 1 ounce of cheese.

Nutrition: Calories: 400; 3 lean protein, 3 Greens.

Broccoli Cheese Soup

Ingredients:
- 3 cups broccoli, chopped (6 Greens)
- 1/8 tsp. salt (1/2 Condiment)
- 1/8 tsp. pepper (1/4 Condiment)
- 1/8 tsp. garlic powder (1/4 Condiment)
- 2 cups chicken broth (2 Condiments)
- 4 light cheese wedges (2 Healthy Fats)
- 1/2 cup reduced-fat shredded cheddar cheese (1/2 Lean)

Directions:

In a pot, add broth, broccoli, salt, pepper, and garlic powder and put it on high heat until it boils. Reduce the heat and simmer for 15 minutes. Add the cheese wedges and stir until melted. Use an immersion blender to smooth the mixture. Pour into 2 bowls and stir in 1/4 cup cheese per bowl.
Servings: 2
Each serving provides 1/4 Lean, 3 Greens, 1.5 Condiments, and 1 Healthy Fat.

Chicken Zucchini Noodle Soup

Ingredients:
- 1 1/4 cups or 162.5 g spiralized zucchini (2 1/2 Greens)
- 1 tsp. olive oil
- 1/2 tsp. minced garlic (1/2 Condiment)
- 1/4 cup celery or 25 g, chopped (1/2 Green)
- 6 oz. cooked chicken breast, skin removed, cut into 1-inch pieces (1 Leaner)
- 2 cups chicken broth (2 Condiments)
- 1/2 tsp. dried basil (1/4 Condiment)
- 1/4 tsp. dried oregano (1/4 Condiment)
- 1/8 tsp. black pepper (1/4 Condiment)

Directions:
On a medium saucepan over medium-high heat. Add olive oil, garlic, and celery. Cook until tender. Add chicken broth, basil, oregano, black pepper, and chicken. Bring to a boil and then reduce heat. Simmer for about 10 minutes. Add the zucchini noodles and cook for 5 more minutes.

Servings: 1
Each serving provides 1 Lean, 3 Greens, 3 Condiments, and 1 Healthy Fat

Chicken and Vegetable Soup

Ingredients:

- 6 oz. chicken breasts, cooked and chopped (1 Leaner Lean)
- 1/2 cup yellow squash, cubed (1 Green)
- 1/2 cup zucchini, cubed (1 Green)
- 1/2 cup green beans, chopped into 1-inch pieces (1 Green)
- 2 cups chicken broth (2 Condiments)
- 1/4 tsp. oregano leaves (1/4 Condiment)
- 1/4 tsp. basil leaves (1/8 Condiment)
- 1/8 tsp. black pepper (1/4 Condiment)

Directions:
Combine all ingredients in a saucepan and bring to a boil. Cover and simmer for 10.

Servings: 1
Each serving provides 1 Lean, 3 Greens, and 3 Condiments

Beef Taco Soup

Ingredients:
- 2 lbs. 95 to 97% lean ground beef (4 Leaner)
- 4 1/2 ounces or 9 tbsp. reduced-fat cream cheese (4 1/2 Healthy Fats)
- 2 cans tomatoes (5 Greens)
- 1 tbsp. low sodium taco seasoning (6 Condiments)
- 2 tsp. Ranch seasoning mix (4 Condiments)
- 4 cups low sodium chicken broth (4 Condiments)
- 3/4 cup 2% plain Greek yogurt (1/2 Leaner)
- 1/2 cup reduced-fat cheddar cheese, shredded (1/2 Lean)
- 5 tbsp. fresh cilantro, chopped (1/3 Condiment)

Directions:
On a skillet over high heat cook the ground beef until brown. In the meantime, place cream cheese, canned tomatoes, taco seasoning, and ranch seasoning in a slow cooker. Drain grease from meat and put it in the slow cooker. Pour chicken broth over the mixture. Cook on LOW for 4 hours or on HIGH for 2 hours. Before serving, stir in Greek yogurt. Divide portions into 5 bowls and top with cheddar cheese.

Servings: 5
Each serving provides 1 Leaner, 1 Green, 3 Condiments, and 1 Healthy Fat

Curry Roasted Cauliflower Soup

Ingredients:
- 1 ½ cups roasted cauliflower florets (3 Greens)
- ¼ teaspoon curry powder (½ Condiment)
- ¼ teaspoon cumin (¼ Condiment)
- ⅛ tsp. garlic powder (¼ Condiment)
- ⅛ tsp. onion powder (¼ Condiment)
- ⅛ tsp. salt (½ Condiment)
- 1 cup vegetable broth (1 Condiment)
- ½ cup water
- ¼ cup lite coconut milk (1 Healthy Fat)
- Garnish: 1 tbsp. chopped cilantro (1/16 Condiment)

Directions:
To roast cauliflower, heat oven to 450°F. Place cauliflower florets on a baking sheet lined with parchment paper. Bake for 25 minutes, turning the florets once. In a small saucepan, add broth, ½ cup water, roasted cauliflower, curry powder, cumin, garlic powder, onion powder, and salt. Bring to a boil and cook on low for 10 minutes. Stir in coconut milk.
Smooth the mixture with an immersion blender and top with cilantro.

Servings: 1
Each serving provides 3 Greens, 3 Condiments, and 1 Healthy Fat

Egg Drop Soup

Ingredients:
- 1 cup chicken broth (1 Condiment)
- 1/4 teaspoon soy sauce (1/12 Condiment)
- 1/4 teaspoon sesame oil (1/4 Healthy Fat)
- 1 beaten egg (1/3 lean)

Directions:
Bring to a boil broth, soy sauce and, sesame oil. Stir gently and pour in the beaten egg. Cook for about 1 minute.

Servings: 1
Each serving provides 1/3 Lean, 1.1 Condiments and 1/4 Healthy Fat

Meatball Soup

Ingredients:
- 5 Frozen Meatballs from your grocery store (1 Lean)
- 1 cup diced tomatoes, (2 Greens)
- 1/2 cup zucchini, chopped (1 Green)
- 1 1/2 cups low sodium beef broth (1 1/2 Condiments)
- 1/8 tsp. black pepper (1/4 Condiment)
- 1/2 tsp. Dried Basil Leaves (1/4 Condiment)

Directions:
Heat meatballs in the microwave for 2 minutes. Cut the meatballs in 4. Use an immersion blender to puree the diced tomatoes. Combine now all the ingredients in a saucepan and bring it to a boil. Simmer for 15 minutes.

Servings: 1
Each serving provides 1 Lean, 3 Greens and 2 Condiments

Cauliflower Soup

Ingredients:

- 1 1/2 cups cauliflower, fresh (3 Greens)
- 1 cup chicken broth (1 Condiment)
- 2 wedges light cheese (1 Healthy Fat)
- 1/8 tsp. salt (1/2 Condiment)
- 1/8 tsp. black pepper (1/4 Condiment)
- 1 tbsp. fresh chives, chopped (1/4 Condiment)
- 2 tbsp. reduced-fat cheddar cheese (1/8 Lean)
- 1 tbsp. of Turkey Bacon bits (1 Condiment)

Directions:
Bring to a boil the cauliflower and broth. Reduce heat to a simmer, cover, and cook until the cauliflower for 15 minutes. Remove from heat and add light cheese wedges, salt and pepper. Smooth it with an immersion blender. Pour into bowls and add cheddar cheese, bacon bits, and chives.

Servings: 1
Each serving provides 1/8 Lean, 3 Greens, 3 Condiments and 1 Healthy Fat

Roasted Squash Soup

Ingredients:
- 3 cups roasted squash (6 Greens)
- 2 cups chicken broth (2 Condiments)
- 1 1/2 cups unsweetened cashew milk (1 1/2 Condiments)
- 1/2 tsp. garlic powder (1 Condiment)
- 1/4 tsp. onion powder (1/2 Condiment)
- 1/2 tsp. dried parsley (1/6 Condiment)
- 1/8 tsp. black pepper (1/4 Condiment)

Directions:
In a medium saucepan, combine all ingredients over medium high heat. Bring to a boil and then let simmer for 10 minutes. Smooth it with an immersion blender.
Servings: 2
Each serving provides 3 Greens and 2.7 Condiments

 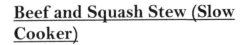 

Beef and Squash Stew (Slow Cooker)

Ingredients:
- 29 oz. raw Beef Stew Meat (4 Leans)
- 4 cups Squash (8 Greens)
- 3 cups low sodium Beef Broth (3 Condiments)
- 1 cup Rao's Marinara Sauce (4 Greens)
- 1 tsp. Garlic Powder (2 Condiments)
- 1 tsp. Italian Seasoning (2 Condiments)
- Salt and Pepper to taste, but don't forget to count them as Condiments!

Directions:
Combine all ingredients in a slow cooker. Cook on Low for 7 hours or High for 4 to 5 hours.

Servings: 4
Each serving provides 1 Lean, 3 Greens, and 1.75 Condiments.

Creamy Cauliflower Soup

Preparation Time: 20 minutes
Cooking Time: 30 minutes
Servings: 4

Ingredients:
- 5 cups cauliflower rice
- 8 oz. cheddar cheese (grated)
- 2 cups unsweetened almond milk
- 2 cups vegetable stock
- 2 tbsp. water
- 1 small onion (chopped)
- 2 garlic cloves (minced)
- 1 tbsp. olive oil
- Pepper
- Salt

Directions:
1) Heat olive oil in a large stockpot over medium heat.

2) Add onion and garlic and cook for 1-2 minutes.
3) Add cauliflower rice and water. Cover and cook for 5-7 minutes.
4) Now add vegetable stock and almond milk and stir well. Bring to boil.
5) Turn heat to low and simmer for 5 minutes.
6) Turn off the heat. Slowly add cheddar cheese and stir until smooth.
7) Season the soup with pepper and salt.
8) Stir well and serve hot.

Nutrition: Calories 214; 1 Lean, 1 healthy fat.

Delicious Zucchini Quiche

Preparation Time: 20 minutes
Cooking Time: 30 minutes
Servings: 4

Ingredients:
- 6 eggs
- 2 medium zucchini (shredded)
- ½ tsp. dried basil
- 2 garlic cloves (minced)
- 1 tbsp. dry onion (minced)
- 2 tbsp. parmesan cheese (grated)
- 2 tbsp. fresh parsley (chopped)
- ½ cup olive oil
- 1 cup cheddar cheese (shredded)
- ¼ cup coconut flour
- ¾ cup almond flour
- ½ tsp. Salt

Directions:
1) Preheat the oven to 350°F. Grease 9-inch pie dish and set aside.
2) Squeeze out excess liquid from zucchini.
3) Add all ingredients into the large bowl and mix until well combined. Pour into the prepared pie dish.
4) Bake in preheated oven for 45-60 minutes or until set.

Nutrition: Calories 288; 1 lean protein, 2 healthy fat, 1 Green.

Turkey Spinach Egg Muffins

Preparation Time: 20 minutes
Cooking Time: 40 minutes
Servings: 4

Ingredients:
- 5 egg whites
- 2 eggs
- ¼ cup cheddar cheese (shredded)
- ¼ cup spinach (chopped)
- ¼ cup milk
- 3 lean breakfast turkey sausage
- Pepper, Salt

Directions:

1) Preheat the oven to 350° F. Grease muffin tray cups and set aside.
2) In a pan, brown the turkey sausage links over medium-high heat until sausage is brown from all the sides.
3) Cut sausage in ½-inch pieces and set aside.
4) In a large bowl, whisk together eggs, egg whites, milk, pepper, and salt. Stir in spinach.
5) Pour egg mixture into the prepared muffin tray.
6) Divide sausage and cheese evenly between each muffin cup.
7) Bake it in preheated oven for 20 minutes or until muffins are set.

Nutrition: Calories: 123; 3 lean protein, 1 Green.

EGGS

Egg Drop Soup

Ingredients:
- 1 cup chicken broth (1 Condiment)
- 1/4 teaspoon soy sauce (1/12 Condiment)
- 1/4 teaspoon sesame oil (1/4 Healthy Fat)
- 1 egg, beaten (1/3 lean)
- 1 tsp. fresh chopped chives (1/12 Condiment)

Directions:
Bring to a boil broth, soy sauce, and sesame oil. Stir gently and pour in the beaten egg. Cook for about 1 minute. Season with chives before serving.

Servings: 1
Each serving provides 1/3 Lean, 1.2 Condiments and 1/4 Healthy Fat

Egg Foo Young

Ingredients:
- 2 teaspoon sesame oil, divided (2 Healthy Fats)
- 1/4 cup chopped green onion (1/2 Green)
- 1/4 cup chopped celery (1/2 Green)
- 1 cup cabbage, shredded (2 Greens)
- 3.5 oz. shrimp cooked (1/2 Leanest Lean)
- 1 tbsp. lite soy sauce (1 Condiment)
- 1/8 tsp. garlic powder (1/4 Condiment)
- 1/8 tsp. onion powder (1/4 Condiment)
- 1/8 tsp. ground red pepper (1/4 Condiment)
- 1 cup egg beaters (1/2 Leanest Lean)

Directions:
Lightly cook celery, cabbage, and onion with the sesame oil for 2-3 minutes. Add shrimps roughly chopped, soy sauce, garlic powder, and onion powder. Stir, remove from heat,

and transfer to a bowl. Add another tbsp. of sesame oil to the pan and add eggbeaters. Quickly stir and add the shrimp/vegetable mixture. Continue cooking until eggs are done

Servings: 1
Each serving provides 1 Leanest Lean, 3 Greens, 2 Healthy Fats, and 1.75 Condiments.

Egg White Sausage Biscuits

Ingredients:
- 2 large egg whites
- 1 turkey sausage cooked

Directions:
Place 2 pastry rings in a skillet over medium-high heat. Spray with cooking spray and place the egg whites inside of them. Pour a little bit of water to create steam. Cover the skillet and let cook for 2 minutes. Remove the eggs from the skilled. Place heated sausage between the egg whites.

Servings: 1
Each serving provides 1/3 Lean

Cauliflower Breakfast Casserole

Ingredients:
- 8 oz. turkey sausage, cooked
- 1/4 cup onion, chopped
- 2 cups cauliflower florets
- 1/2 tsp. seasonings of your choice
- 1/4 tsp. salt
- 1/4 tsp. fresh ground black pepper
- 6 slices turkey bacon, cooked and cut into pieces
- 2 cups 2% Mexican style shredded cheese
- 8 large eggs
- 16 oz. egg whites or egg beaters
- 1/4 cup unsweetened almond milk

Directions:
Preheat oven to 350°F. Spray a 9x13 baking tray with cooking spray. On a skillet at medium heat, spray some Pam and sauté cauliflower and onions. Add the sausage chopped, season with the desired seasonings, and spread the vegetable in the baking tray. Sprinkle the turkey bacon chops and cheddar cheese. In a bowl whisk eggs, egg whites, and almond milk and pour the mixture into the tray. Bake for 45 minutes.

Servings: 8
Each serving provides 1 Lean, 1/2 Green, and 1 Condiment

Italian Sausage Sweet Red Pepper Quiche

Ingredients:
- 6 ounces cooked turkey sausage, drained fat (1 Lean)
- 4 eggs (1 1/2 Lean with 2 egg whites)
- 2 egg whites
- 1 1/2 cups sweet red bell pepper, chopped (3 Greens)
- 1 cup unsweetened almond milk (1 Condiment)
- 1 cup shredded 2% sharp cheddar cheese (1 Lean)
- 1/4 tsp. salt (1 Condiment)
- 1/4 tsp. pepper (1/2 Condiment)
- 2 tbsp. reduced-fat grated parmesan cheese (1 Condiment)
- 1 Light cauliflower pizza crust of your choice (1/2 Lean, 3 Greens)

Directions:
Preheat oven to 350°F. Remove cauliflower pizza crust from freezer to thaw. Spray Pam on a 9" pie dish and place the pizza crust in it. Bake for 8 minutes. In the meantime, whisk together eggs, egg whites, and almond milk. Add cheddar, chopped pepper, and chopped sausage and season with salt,

pepper, and parmesan. Pour the mix into the pie dish. Bake 50 minutes more.

Servings: 8
Each serving provides 1 Lean, 1 1/2 Green and 1 Condiment

Kabocha, Sausage and Egg Breakfast Casserole

Ingredients:
- 2 1/2 cups kabocha squash, shredded (5 Greens)
- 1/2 cup red bell pepper, diced (1 Green)
- 6 ounces turkey sausage crumbles (1 Lean)
- 12 eggs (4 Leans)
- 1/2 cup unsweetened almond milk (1/2 Condiment)
- 1 tsp. dried sage (1/2 Condiment)
- 1/2 tsp. salt (2 Condiments)
- 1/2 tsp. ground black pepper (1 Condiment)
- 1 cup 2% reduced-fat sharp cheddar cheese (1 Lean)

Directions:
Preheat oven to 350°F. Spray a 9" x 13" glass casserole with cooking spray. Wash, cut the kabocha squash in half, and scoop the seeds out. Cut the halves into wedges and remove the skin. Cut the wedges into large chunks so they can fit into the tube of the food processor and then shred roughly. Spread 2 1/2 cups of shredded kabocha squash in the casserole dish and sprinkle the diced red bell pepper, turkey sausage crumbles. Prepare a mix of eggs, almond milk, sage, salt, and pepper and pour it into the casserole. Sprinkle cheese on top and bake uncovered for 45 minutes.

Servings: 6
Each serving provides 1 Lean, 1 Green, and 1 Condiment.

Mexican Beef Egg Burrito

Ingredients:
- 2.5 oz. 93% lean ground beef, cooked (1/2 Lean)
- 1 light cheese wedge (1 Condiment)
- 1/4 cup diced tomatoes (1/2 Green)
- 1/2 tsp. taco seasoning (1 Condiment)
- 1 cup egg whites (1/2 Lean)
- 1 tbsp. chipotle salsa (1 Condiment)

Directions:
Cook in a skillet ground beef, tomatoes, cheese, and taco seasoning. Set aside once cooked. Spray a non-stick skillet with cooking spray and prepare an omelet with the eggbeaters. Place the omelet on a plate and add the ground beef mixture to the center. Fold like a burrito and top with salsa.

Servings: 1
Each serving provides 1 Lean, 1/2 of 1 Green, and 3 Condiments

Spinach Cheddar Quiche

Ingredients:
- 4 eggs (1 1/2 Leans with egg whites)
- 2 egg whites
- 1 1/2 cups cooked spinach (3 Greens)
- 1 cup unsweetened almond milk (1 Condiment)
- 1 cup 2% sharp cheddar shredded cheese (1 Lean)
- 1/4 tsp. salt (1 Condiment)
- 1/4 tsp. pepper (1/2 Condiment)
- 1/4 tsp. garlic powder (1/2 Condiment)
- 1/4 tsp. onion powder (1/2 Condiment)
- 1/4 cup reduced-fat feta cheese (2 Condiments)
- 1 frozen cauliflower pizza crust (1/2 Lean, 3 Greens)

Directions:
Preheat oven to 350 °F. Remove pizza crust from freezer to thaw. Whisk eggs, egg whites, and unsweetened almond milk together. Add cheddar cheese, feta cheese, and cooked spinach and season with salt, pepper, garlic powder, and onion powder. Spray Pam in a 9" pie pan and place the pizza crust in and place in the oven for 5 minutes. Remove from oven and pour the egg mixture. Bake 45 minutes more.

Servings: 3
Each serving provides 1 Lean, 2 Greens and 2 Condiments

Thai Eggs

Ingredients:
- 3 eggs (1 Lean)
- 2 tsp. fish sauce (2/3 Condiment)
- 1/8 tsp. pepper (1/4 Condiment)
- Cooking Spray

Directions:
Whisk together eggs, fish sauce, and pepper. Spray Pam in a frying pan over medium-high heat. Pour the egg mixture and prepare the omelet

Servings: 3
Each serving provides 1 Lean and 1 Condiment

Crustless Turkey Cheddar Quiche

Ingredients:
- 7 ounces turkey, cooked and cubed (1 Leanest)
- ⅔ cup reduced-fat cheddar cheese (⅔ Lean)
- 1 tbsp. butter (2 Healthy Fats)
- ¼ cup onion (4 Condiments)
- 1 tsp. minced garlic (1 Condiment)

- 1 ½ cups fresh broccoli florets cooked, chopped finely (3 Greens)
- 4 eggs (1 ⅓ Lean)
- ½ cup unsweetened almond milk (½ Condiment)
- ¼ tsp. salt (1 Condiment)
- ¼ tsp. pepper (½ Condiment)

Directions:
Preheat 375°F. Melt butter in a skillet over medium-high heat. Cook onion and garlic for 5 minutes and put them in a 9" pie dish. Add turkey, cheese, and broccoli. In the meantime, beat eggs, almond milk, salt, and pepper. Pour the mixture over turkey, cheese, and broccoli. Bake 40 to 45 minutes.

Servings: 3
Each serving provides 1 Lean, 1 Green, 2 ⅓ Condiments, and ⅔ Healthy Fat (for turkey)

Vegetable Quiche

Ingredients:
- 1 cup egg beaters (1/2 leanest)
- ½ cup part-skim 2 % Mozzarella cheese for pizza (1/2 lean)
- 1/2 cup tomato, chopped (1 green)
- 1/2 cup broccoli, chopped (1 green)
- 1/2 cup zucchini, chopped (1 green)
- 2 cheese wedge (2 healthy fat)
- 1/4 tsp. salt (1 condiment)
- 1/4 tsp. pepper (1/2 condiment)
- 1/4 tsp. onion powder (1/2 condiment)

Directions:
Preheat oven to 375°F. Spray Pam on a baking dish. Mix all the ingredients in a bowl and pour the mixture into the pan. Bake for 30 minutes.

Servings: 1
Each serving provides 1 Lean, 3 Greens, 2 Condiments, and 2 Healthy Fat.

Spinach Tomato Frittata

Preparation Time: 20 minutes
Cooking Time: 40 minutes
Servings: 4

Ingredients:
- 12 eggs
- 2 cups baby spinach, shredded
- 1/4 cup sun-dried tomatoes (sliced)
- 1/2 tsp. dried basil
- 1/4 cup parmesan cheese (grated)
- Pepper
- Salt

Directions:
1) Preheat the oven to 425°F. Grease an oven-safe pan and set aside.
2) In a large bowl, whisk eggs with pepper and salt. Add remaining ingredients and stir to combine.
3) Pour the egg mixture into the prepared pan and bake for 20 minutes.
4) Slice and serve.

Nutrition: Calories 116; 1 serving leaner protein, 2 Greens.

PIZZAS, WRAPS AND BREADS

Beef and Cheddar Pizza

Ingredients:
- 1.25 ounces cooked beef with 2 tbsp. sugar free bbq sauce (1/4 Lean, 2 Condiments)
- 1/4 cup reduced-fat sharp cheddar cheese (1/4 Lean)
- 1 Lite Cauliflower Foods crust of your favorite grocery store (1/2 Lean, 3 Greens)

To make Shredded Beef:
- 3 pound chuck roast
- 1 cup diet root beer
- Sugar-Free BBQ Sauce

Directions:
Cook on low for 8 hours the roast in the slow cooker with one cup of diet root beer. Drain it and shred with a fork. Measure out 1.25 ounces of cooked beef and add 2 tbsp. sugar free BBQ Sauce and set aside. Bake crust for 10 minutes at 400 degrees. Let cool ten minutes. Add shredded BBQ beef to the crust. Sprinkle 1/4 cup shredded cheddar on top and bake for five more minutes.

Servings: 1
Each serving provides 1 Lean, 3 Greens, and 2 Condiment

Chicken Pizza

Ingredients:
Crust
- 1/4 cup Reduced-fat Mozzarella (1/4 Lean)
- 1/4 cup eggbeater (1/8 Lean)
- 1 cup grated raw cauliflower (2 Greens)

Toppings
- 2.25 oz. chicken breasts, cooked and chopped (3/8 Lean)
- 1/4 cup Reduced-fat 2% Mozzarella Cheese (1/4 Lean)
- 1/2 cup of your favorite veggies - I used broccoli (1 Green)
- 3 tbsp. sugar-free BBQ Sauce (3 Condiments)

Directions:
Place parchment paper on a sheet and spray with cooking spray. Mix grated cauliflower, eggbeaters, and mozzarella. Spoon mixture on the parchment paper and use the back of a spoon to thin the mixture and form a circle. Bake in a preheated oven for 30 minutes at 425°F, then flip it and bake for another 8 minutes. Spread BBQ sauce over crust. Top with chicken and veggies. Sprinkle 1/4 cup cheese over the top. Put it again in the oven for 5 minutes more.

Servings: 1
Each serving provides 1 Lean, 3 Greens, and 3 Condiments

Burger Pizza

Ingredients:
- 1 Lite Cauliflower pizza crust of your favorite grocery store (1/2 Lean, 3 Greens)
- 1.75 oz. 99% ground turkey, seasoned and cooked (1/4 Leanest Lean)
- 1/4 cup reduced-fat sharp cheddar cheese, shredded (1/4 Lean)
- 1/2 cup lettuce, chopped (1/2 Green)
- 1/4 cup tomatoes, chopped (1/2 Green)
- 2 dill pickles, chopped (1 Fueling).

For Dressing:

- 2 tbsp. Light salad Dressing (1 Healthy Fat)
- 1/8 tsp. white wine vinegar
- Light sprinkle of stevia, optional

Directions:
Preheat the oven to 400 degrees and bake the pizza crust for 10 minutes. Let it cool completely after that. Combine the ingredients of the dressing in a small bowl. Put the ground turkey and cheese on top of the crust and bake 5 minutes more. Add lettuce, tomatoes, and pickles. Drizzle dressing mixture on top.

Servings: 2 (half pizza per serving)
Each serving provides 1/2 Lean, 2 Greens, 1/2 Healthy Fat, and 1/2 Fueling

Buffalo Chicken Pizza 1

Ingredients:
Crust:
- 1/4 cup egg beaters (1/8 Lean)
- 1/4 cup reduced-fat cheese (1/4 Lean)
- 1 cup grated, raw cauliflower (2 Greens)

Toppings:
- 2.25 oz. chicken breasts, cooked and chopped (3/8 Lean)
- 2 tbsp. Frank's Hot Sauce (1 Condiment)
- 1 tbsp. reduced-fat ranch dressing (1/2 Healthy Fat)
- 1 tbsp. reduced-fat cream cheese (1 Condiment)
- 1/4 cup reduced-fat cheddar or Mexican cheese (1/4 Lean)

Directions:
Place parchment paper on a sheet and spray with cooking spray. Mix grated cauliflower, egg beaters, and mozzarella. Spoon mixture on the parchment paper and use the back of a spoon to thin the mixture and form a circle. Bake in a preheated oven for 30 minutes at

425°F, then flip it and bake for another 8 minutes. Combine chicken, hot sauce, ranch dressing, and cream cheese and spread the mixture on the crust. Top with 1/4 cup of shredded cheese. Bake for 5 minutes.

Servings: 1
Each serving provides 1 Lean, 2 Greens, 2 Condiments and a 1/2 Healthy Fat

Buffalo Chicken Pizza 2

Ingredients:
- 1 Cauliflower pizza crust of your favorite grocery store (1/2 Lean, 3 Greens)
- 1/4 cup reduced-fat mozzarella cheese (1/4 Lean)
- 1.5 oz. skinless grilled chicken breast (1/4 Lean)
- 1 Tablespoon reduced-fat cream cheese (1 Condiments)
- 3 Tablespoon hot sauce (1 1/2 Condiments)
- Garnish: Green onions, sliced

Directions:
Preheat the oven to 400 degrees and bake the pizza crust for 10 minutes. Let it cool completely after that. Combine well chicken and 1 tbsp. of hot sauce in a bowl. Mix cream cheese with 2 tbsp. of hot sauce until smooth. Spread all over the crust and add chicken and mozzarella on top. Bake for 5 minutes more and garnish with sliced green onions.

Servings: 1
Each serving provides 1 Lean, 3 Greens, and 2.5 Condiments

Cauliflower Crisps

Ingredients:
- 1 Cauliflower pizza crust of your favorite grocery store (1/2 Lean, 3 Greens)
For the Dip:

- 1/4 cup 2% plain Greek yogurt (1/6 Lean)
- 1/2 tsp. Bagel Seasoning (2 Condiments)

Directions:
Preheat oven to 400 degrees and cut the crust into triangles. Bake them for 10 minutes. While you let them cool mix the bagel dressing with the Greek yogurt to create the dip.

Servings: 1
Each serving provides 2/3 Lean, 3 Greens, and 2 Condiments

Cauliflower Fries

Ingredients:
- 2 Cauliflower flatbreads of your favorite grocery store (1/3 Lean, 2 Greens)
- Optional: 1 tbsp. reduced sugar ketchup (1 Condiment)

Directions:
Preheat oven to 400 degrees and cook the flatbreads for 5 minutes. Remove from oven and cut into sticks to create fries. Place them in the oven again for 5 minutes more to make them crunchy. Dip them in ketchup.
Servings: 1
Each serving provides 1/3 Lean, 2 Greens, and 1 Condiment

Cauliflower Bread Sticks

Ingredients:
- 1 cup raw grated cauliflower (2 Greens)
- 1/4 cup liquid egg substitute (1.3 Condiments)
- 1 cup shredded reduced-fat mozzarella cheese (1 Lean)
- 1/8 tsp. Garlic salt (1/2 Condiment)
- 1/4 tsp. dried Basil (1/8 Condiment)
- 1/4 tsp. dried Oregano (1/4 Condiment)

Marinara Sauce

- 1/2 cup diced tomatoes (1 Green)

Directions:
Blend the diced tomatoes and set them aside. Place parchment paper on a 9 x 5 loaf pan and spray with cooking spray. Mix grated cauliflower, egg substitute, and mozzarella. Spoon mixture on the parchment paper and use the back of a spoon to thin the mixture and cover the loaf. Bake in a preheated oven for 30 minutes at 425°F, then flip it and bake for another 8 minutes. Take out of the oven and with a pizza cutter slice strips. Sprinkle with garlic salt and 1/4 cup 2% reduced-fat mozzarella. Continue baking at 450°F for 10 more minutes. Serve with marinara sauce.

Servings: 1
Each serving provides 1 Lean, 2.25 Condiments and 3 Greens

Cauliflower Lasagna

Ingredients:
- 2 Cauliflower pizza crust of your favorite grocery store (1 Lean, 6 Greens)

For Meat Mixture:
- 1/4 cup Onions, chopped (4 Condiments)
- 1/2 lb. 97% Lean Ground Beef, uncooked (1 Leaner)
- 1/4 tsp. Salt (1 Condiments)
- 1/8 tsp. Black Pepper (1/4 Condiment)
- 1/4 tsp. Garlic Powder (1/2 Condiment)
- 3/4 cup Marinara Sauce (3 Greens)
- 1/2 cup Diced Tomatoes (1 Green)

For Cottage Cheese Mixture:
- 12 oz. 2% Cottage Cheese (1 Leaner)
- 3 tbsp. Egg Beaters (1 Condiment)
- 2 tsp. Dried Parsley (2/3 Condiment)

Additional Toppings:
- 2 cups Fresh Baby Spinach (2 Greens)
- 1/4 cup Fresh Basil, chopped (1/2 Condiment)

- 1 cup Reduced-fat Mozzarella Cheese (1 Lean)
- 1/4 cup Fresh Grated Parmesan Cheese (4 Condiments)

Directions:
Meat Mixture: Sautee onions in the skillet non-stick skillet sprayed with cooking spray 5 minutes. Add the ground beef, salt, black pepper, and garlic powder. Continue cooking until the meat is brown. Drain the fat, stir in the marinara sauce, and diced tomatoes. Cook for five more minutes and set aside. Cottage Cheese Mixture: In a small bowl combine cottage cheese, eggbeaters, and parsley. Set aside. Spinach: Clean spinach and, while leaves are wet, place them in the microwave, covered safe bowl. Steam in the microwave for 2 min. Chop and set aside. Preheat oven to 375 degrees and assemble the lasagna on a dish pie pan, sprayed with cooking spray: layer the meat mix, the cauliflower crusts, cottage cheese, spinach, basil, mozzarella, and parmesan cheese. Make two layers and finish with a meat mixture. Bake for 45 min. and enjoy.

Servings: 4
Each serving provides 1 Lean, 3 Greens, and 3 Condiments

Cauliflower Margherita

Ingredients:
Crust:
- 1 cup (100 g) grated raw cauliflower (2 Greens)
- ¼ cup egg substitute ~ egg whites or egg beaters (1 ⅓ Condiments)
- ½ cup 2% reduced-fat three cheese Mexican blend or mozzarella cheese (½ Lean)

Toppings:

- ½ cup 2% reduced-fat Mozzarella cheese, shredded (½ Lean)
- ½ cup diced tomatoes

Directions:
Place parchment paper on a sheet and spray with cooking spray. Mix grated cauliflower, eggbeaters, and mozzarella. Spoon mixture on the parchment paper and use the back of a spoon to thin the mixture and form a circle. Bake in a preheated oven for 30 minutes at 425°F, then flip it and bake for another 8 minutes. Let cool. Spread tomato sauce and sprinkle ½ cup of cheese on top. Bake for an additional 5 minutes or until cheese is melted. If you are making several cauliflower pizza crusts, you can put the cooled crusts in gallon-sized Ziploc bags to store in the freezer. No need to wrap each one separately.

Servings: 1
Each serving provides ½ a Lean, 2 Greens and 2 Condiments

Chicken Alfredo and Spinach "Pizza"

Ingredients:
Crust
- 1 cup or 100 grams grated raw cauliflower (2 Greens)
- 1/4 cup egg beaters (1/8 Lean)
- 1/4 cup Reduced-fat 2% Mozzarella cheese (2/8 Lean)

Toppings
- 2.25 oz. chicken, cooked and chopped (3/8 Lean)
- 1/4 cup Reduced-fat 2% Mozzarella Cheese (2/8 lean)
- 1/2 cup spinach, cooked, drained and chopped (1 Green)
- 2 tbsp. reduced-fat feta cheese (1 Condiment)

Alfredo Sauce
- 2 Light Garlic and Herb Cheese Wedges (1 Healthy Fat)
- 2 tbsp. unsweetened almond milk (1/8 Condiments)
- 1 tbsp. Reduced-fat Parmesan, grated (1/2 Condiment)

Directions:
Place parchment paper on a sheet and spray with cooking spray. Mix grated cauliflower, eggbeaters, and mozzarella. Spoon mixture on the parchment paper and use the back of a spoon to thin the mixture and form a circle. Bake in a preheated oven for 30 minutes at 425°F, then flip it and bake for another 8 minutes. Let cool. Prepare the Alfredo sauce combining the related ingredients in a small saucepan over low heat. Bring to a boil and stir constantly until it thickens. Remove from heat and stir in chicken. Top the crust with cooked spinach. Then spread the chicken mixture over the spinach. Top with 1/4 cup mozzarella and sprinkle feta cheese on top. Bake for 5 minutes

Servings: 1
Each serving provides 1 Lean, 3 Greens, 1 3/4 Condiments and 1 Healthy Fat

Spaghetti Squash Pizza Crusts

Ingredients:
- 1 cup spaghetti squash, cooked (2 Greens)
- 2 tbsp. egg whites or egg beaters
- 1/4 cup reduced-fat mozzarella cheese (1/4 Lean)
- 1 tbsp. grated Kraft reduced-fat parmesan cheese (1 Condiment)
- 1/4 tsp. Oregano (1/2 Condiment)
- 1/8 tsp. garlic powder (1/4 Condiment)
Directions:
Preheat oven to 400 degrees. Mix spaghetti squash, egg whites, mozzarella, parmesan cheese, oregano, and garlic powder in a small

bowl. Spread spaghetti squash mixture on a baking tray with parchment paper sprayed with cooking spray and form a circle. Bake for 25 minutes and flip the crust. Bake 10 more minutes. Top crust with your favorite toppings and bake an additional 5 minutes.

Servings: 1
Each serving provides 1/4 Lean, 2 Greens, and 2 Condiments

Chicken Ranch Pizza

Ingredients:
- 1 Cauliflower pizza crust of your favorite grocery store (1/2 Lean, 3 Greens)
- 1.5 oz. cooked chicken breasts, chopped (1/4 Lean)
- 1/4 cup reduced-fat mozzarella cheese (1/4 Lean)
- 1 1/2 tbsp. Ranch Dressing (3 Condiments)

Directions:
Bake the crust for 10 min in a preheated oven to 400°F. Let it cool for 5 min. Spread ranch dressing and add chicken and cheese. Bake for 6 minutes more.

Servings: 1
Each serving provides 1 Lean, 3 Greens, and 3 Condiments

Chicken and Feta Flatbreads

Ingredients:
- 2 Cauliflower flatbreads of your favorite grocery store (1/3 Lean, 2 Greens)
- 2 tbsp. marinara sauce (1 Condiment)
- 15 grams raw spinach, chopped (1/2 Green)
- 45 grams tomatoes, diced (1/2 Green)
- 2 ounces cooked chicken, diced (1/3 Leaner)

- 1/3 cup fat reduced mozzarella cheese (1/3 Lean)
- 1 tbsp. sliced red onion (1 Condiment)
- 2 tbsp. reduced-fat feta cheese (1 Condiment)

Directions:
Preheat oven to 375°F. Place flatbreads on a pan with parchment. Bake flatbreads for 10 and then let them cool. Top flatbreads with marinara sauce, spinach, tomatoes, chicken, mozzarella, and red onion. Sprinkle feta cheese on top. Bake for 5 minutes more.

Servings: 1
Each serving provides 1 Lean, 3 Greens, and 3 Condiments.

Basil, Mozzarella and Roasted Tomato Pizza

Ingredients:
- • 1 Cauliflower pizza crust of your favorite grocery store (1/2 Lean, 3 Greens)
- 1 tsp. fresh minced garlic (1 Condiment)
- 1/2 cup 2% reduced-fat mozzarella cheese (1/2 Lean)
- 1/2 cup grape tomatoes cut in halves (1 Green)
- 1/4 cup fresh basil, chopped (1/2 Condiment)
- 1 tbsp. Balsamic Vinegar (3 Condiments)
- Olive oil cooking spray

Directions:
Preheat oven to 400 degrees. Line a baking sheet with parchment paper. Spread the halved tomatoes on it and spray lightly with olive oil cooking spray. Bake for about 15 to 20 minutes. Set aside. Place pizza crust on a tray with parchment paper. Spray the crust with olive oil cooking spray and spread minced garlic on top. Bake for 10 minutes. Let cool and then add mozzarella cheese, fresh basil, and roasted grape tomatoes on

 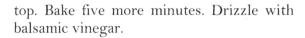 

top. Bake five more minutes. Drizzle with balsamic vinegar.

Servings: 2 (half pizza each serving)
Each serving provides 1/2 Lean, 2 Greens, and 2.25 Condiments (Half the pizza)

Beef and Pepper Pizza

Ingredients:
- 1 Cauliflower pizza crust of your favorite grocery store (1/2 Lean, 3 Greens)
- 1.5 ounces 95 to 97% lean cooked ground beef (1/4 Lean)
- 1/4 cup reduced-fat mozzarella cheese (1/4 Lean)
- 2 tbsp. marinara sauce (1 Condiment)
- 1 ounce sliced banana peppers (1 Fueling)

Directions:
Preheat oven to 400 degrees. Line a baking sheet with parchment paper and bake the crust for 10 min.
Let cool and spread marinara sauce on it. Then sprinkle cooked ground beef and mozzarella cheese over cooled crust and top with pepper slices. Bake for 5 min more

Servings: 1
Each serving provides 1 Lean, 3 Greens, 1 Condiment, and 1 Fueling

Mexican Pizza

Ingredients:
- 1 Cauliflower pizza crust of your favorite grocery store (1/2 Lean, 3 Greens)
- 1.5 oz. 93% ground beef seasoned with taco seasoning (1/4 Lean)
- 1/4 cup reduced-fat Mexican style cheese, shredded (1/4 Lean)
- 2 tbsp. Trader Joe's Cilantro Dressing, divided (2 Condiments)

Directions:
Preheat oven to 400 degrees. Line a baking sheet with parchment paper and bake the crust for 10 min. Let cool and spread 1 tbsp. of Cilantro Dressing over crust. Sprinkle seasoned ground beef, cheese, and jalapenos over crust. Bake for 5 to 6 minutes or until cheese has melted.

Servings: 1
Each serving provides 1 Lean, 3 Greens, and 2 Condiments for the entire pizza

Mini Mexican Pizzas

Ingredients:
- 2 Cauliflower flatbreads of your favorite grocery store (1/3 Lean, 2 Greens)
- 2 ounces 95 to 97 % lean ground beef, cooked (1/3 Lean)
- 1/4 tsp. taco seasoning (1/2 Condiment)
- 1/3 cup reduced-fat cheddar cheese (1/3 Lean)
- 1/2 cup shredded lettuce (1/2 Green)
- 1/4 cup diced tomatoes (1/2 Green)
- 2 tbsp. light sour cream (2 Condiments)
- 1/2 ounce chopped jarred jalapenos (1/2 Condiment)

Directions:
Preheat oven to 375 degrees. Line a baking sheet with parchment paper, bake the flatbreads for 14 min., and then let them cool. Season beef with taco seasoning and top each flatbread with half of the beef and shredded cheese. Bake for an additional 4 to 5 min. Sprinkle lettuce, tomatoes, sour cream, and jalapenos on top of each flatbread.

Servings: 1 (2 mini pizzas)
Each serving provides 1 Lean, 3 Greens, and 3 Condiments for both pizzas

Meat Crust Pizza

Ingredients:
- 9 oz. 93% lean ground beef, cooked (2 Leans with the 1 oz. of turkey pepperoni)
- 2 cups shredded reduced-fat mozzarella cheese (2 Leans)
- 1/4 tsp. salt (1 Condiment)
- 1/4 tsp. garlic powder (1/2 Condiment)
- 1/4 tsp. onion powder (1/2 Condiment)
- 1/2 tsp. Italian seasoning (1 Condiment)
- 1 tbsp. grated reduced-fat parmesan cheese (1/2 Condiment)
- 1 cup Diced Tomatoes (2 Greens)
- 1/4 cup red bell peppers (1/2 Green)
- 1/4 cup green bell peppers (1/2 Green)
- 1/2 cup zucchini, chopped (1 Green)
- 1 oz. turkey pepperoni slices

Directions:
Mix ground beef and 1 cup of mozzarella in a bowl. Add salt, garlic powder, onion powder, Italian seasoning, and parmesan cheese until combined. Spread the mixture into a circle on a baking tray with parchment paper. Blend the tomatoes to create a smooth sauce and put it on top of the meat. Top with 1 cup of mozzarella, red peppers, green peppers, zucchini, and turkey pepperoni. Bake for about 25 minutes.

Servings: 4
Each serving provides 1 Lean, 1 Green, and 1 Condiment.

Pulled BBQ Chicken Pizza

Ingredients:
- • 1 Cauliflower pizza crust of your favorite grocery store (1/2 Lean, 3 Greens)
- 6 ounces Prepared Pulled BBQ Chicken ~ Recipe Below (1 Lean, 3 Condiments)
- 1/2 cup 2% Sharp Cheddar Cheese, Shredded (1/2 Lean)

For the Slaw:
- 1 1/2 cup Shredded Cabbage (3 Greens)
- 2 tbsp. Reduced-fat Mayo (2 Healthy Fats)
- 1/2 tsp. Apple Cider Vinegar
- 1/2 Packet Stevia, or to taste (1/2 Condiment)

For the Slow Cooker Pulled BBQ Chicken:
- 36 ounces Chicken Breasts (4 Leans)
- 12 ounces Diet Root Beer
- 3/4 cup Sugar-Free BBQ Sauce (12 Condiments)

Directions:
Pulled BBQ Chicken: Place chicken and root beer in the slow cooker. Add seasoning such as salt, pepper, garlic powder, etc. Cook for 6 hours at LOW. Drain the chicken and shred it with a fork. Add BBQ sauce and set aside.
Slaw: Place the shredded cabbage in a small bowl with mayo, apple cider vinegar and set aside.
Pizza: Preheat oven to 400 degrees. Line a baking sheet with parchment paper and bake the crust for 5min. Top pizza crust with 6 ounces of pulled BBQ chicken. Sprinkle shredded cheese on top and bake for 12 minutes. Top with slaw.

Servings: 2 (1 serving = half pizza)
Each serving provides 1 Lean, 3 Greens, 1.75 Condiments, and 1 Healthy Fat

Quesadillas

Ingredients:
- • 1 Cauliflower pizza crust of your favorite grocery store (1/2 Lean, 3 Greens)
- 1/2 cup 2% Mexican style cheese (1/2 Lean)
- 2 tbsp. sour cream (2 Condiments)
- 1 ounce jalapenos, jarred (1 Fueling)

- 1 tbsp. red salsa (1 Condiment)

Directions:
Cut crust in half. Spray a non-stick skillet with cooking spray. Cook the crust over medium heat.
Place cheese on half the crust and then place the other half on top. Cook for a few minutes on each side. Serve with sour cream, jalapenos, and salsa.

Servings: 1
Each serving provides 1 Lean, 3 Greens, 3 Condiments, and 1 Fueling.

Teriyaki BBQ Chicken Pizza

Ingredients:
- 1 Cauliflower pizza crust of your favorite grocery store (1/2 Lean, 3 Greens)
- 1.5 ounces cooked chicken breasts, diced (1/4 Lean)
- 1/4 cup reduced-fat sharp cheddar cheese (1/4 Lean)
- 2 tbsp. sugar-free BBQ sauce (2 Condiments)
- 1 tsp. teriyaki sauce (1 Condiment)

Directions:
Preheat oven to 400 degrees. Line a baking sheet with parchment paper and bake the crust for 10minutes. Sprinkle chicken and cheese on cooled crust. Combine BBQ sauce and teriyaki sauce in a small bowl and drizzle it over pizza. Bake for 5 minutes more

Servings: 1
Each serving provides 1 Lean, 3 Greens, and 3 Condiments for the entire pizza

Thai Peanut Chicken "Pizza"

Ingredients:
For the Crust
- 1 cup raw Cauliflower, grated or 100 grams (2 Greens)
- 1/4 cup Egg Beaters (1/8 Lean)
- 1/4 cup 2% Reduced-fat Mozzarella Cheese, shredded (2/8 Lean)

Peanut Sauce
- 2 tbsp. powdered peanut butter (1 Snack)
- 2 tbsp. Sesame Ginger Dressing (1 Condiment)

Toppings:
- 1 tbsp. Low Sodium Soy Sauce (1 Condiment)
- 4 oz. raw Chicken to yield 2.25 oz. Chicken (3/8 Lean)
- 1/4 cup 2% Reduced-fat Mozzarella Cheese (2/8 Lean)
- 1/4 cup or 26 grams Bean Sprouts (1/2 Green)
- 2 tbsp. Red Pepper or 18.6 grams, thinly sliced (1/4 Green)
- 2 tbsp. Green Onions or 12.5 grams, thinly sliced (1/4 Green)
- 2 tbsp. Cilantro, chopped (1/8 Condiment)

Directions:
Marinade for 5 hours chicken in soy sauce. Drain the chicken, grill it and chop it into small pieces. In the meantime, preheat the oven to 425 degrees. Mix grated cauliflower, eggbeaters, and 1/4 cup cheese. Spoon the mixture on a prepared pan with parchment paper. Use the back of a spoon to thin out the mixture and form a circle. Bake for 30 minutes. Flip the pizza crust over and bake for an additional 10 minutes. In a separate bowl, combine powdered peanut butter with Sesame Ginger Dressing. Add the chicken and stir. Spread the chicken mixture over the

top of cooked pizza crust, top with veggies, and sprinkle 1/4 cup cheese over the top. Cook in the oven for 5 more minutes.

Servings: 1
Each serving provides 1 Lean, 3 Greens, 2.12 Condiments, and 1 Snack

Pizza Bread

Ingredients:
- 1 Cream of Tomato Soup (1 Fueling)
- 1/4 tsp. Baking Powder (1/2 Condiment)
- 2 tbsp. Water

Options:
- 1/4 cup shredded reduced-fat cheese (1/4 Lean)
- 1 Light Cheese Wedge (1 Condiment)

Directions:
Preheat oven to 425 degrees. Put parchment paper on a baking tray. Mix soup, baking powder, seasonings, and water in a bowl. Spread the mixture on the baking tray and form a circle. Bake for 5 minutes and then flip it. Add cheese and cook for 5 more minutes.

Servings: 1
Each serving provides 1 Fueling and 1/2 of a Condiment.

White Pizza

Ingredients:
- 1 Cauliflower pizza crust of your favorite grocery store (1/2 Lean, 3 Greens)
- 1/4 cup part-skim ricotta cheese (1/4 Lean)
- 1/4 cup reduced-fat mozzarella cheese (1/4 Lean)
- 2 tbsp. reduced-fat feta cheese (1 Condiment)
- 1 tbsp. grated reduced-fat parmesan cheese (1/2 Condiment)

- 2 tbsp. chopped fresh basil (1/4 Condiment)
- 1/2 tsp. Italian Seasoning (1 Condiment)

Directions:
Bake pizza crust for 10 min. in a preheated oven at 400°F. Thinly spread ricotta cheese on crust, well cooled. Then sprinkle mozzarella, feta, parmesan, basil, and Italian seasoning on top. Bake for an additional 5 minutes.

Servings: 1
Each serving provides 1 Lean, 3 Greens, and 3 Condiments for the entire pizza

Zucchini Wraps

Ingredients:
- 4 cups shredded zucchini
- 1 egg, beaten
- 1/2 cup grated reduced-fat parmesan cheese
- 1 packet Branded Honey Mustard Onion Sticks
- 1/2 tsp. black pepper ~ I used 1/4 tsp.
- 1/4 tsp. salt
- 1/4 tsp. garlic powder
- 1/4 tsp. cumin

Directions:
Preheat oven to 425 degrees. Mix zucchini, egg, parmesan, the Branded fueling, and spices in a large bowl until mixed thoroughly. Drop 1 cup of mixture on a prepared baking tray with parchment paper and cooking spray. Spread the mix as thin as possible, forming large circles. Bake for 25 minutes and let cool. Carefully peel the shells from the parchment paper and enjoy!

Servings: 4
Each serving provides 2 Greens, 1/4 Fueling or 3/4 Healthy Fat and 2 Condiments

Zucchini Pizza Pot

Ingredients:
- 4 cups shredded zucchini (8 Greens)
- 2 eggs (⅔ Lean)
- ½ cup fresh grated parmesan cheese (8 Condiments)
- 1 ⅓ cup reduced-fat Mozzarella cheese (1 ⅓ Lean)
- 1 cup reduced-fat cheddar cheese (1 Lean)
- 1 ½ lbs. 90 to 94% lean ground beef (3 Leans)
- ½ cup chopped onions (8 Condiments)
- 1 tsp. minced garlic (1 Condiment)
- 1 ¾ cups marinara sauce (7 Greens)
- 1 ½ cups chopped bell peppers (3 Greens)

Directions:
Preheat oven to 400 degrees.

Place shredded zucchini on a clean kitchen towel and let it sit for 30 minutes. Squeeze out moisture. Combine squeezed zucchini, eggs, parmesan cheese, ⅔ cup Mozzarella cheese, and ½ cup cheddar cheese in a large bowl. Put the mixture into an oiled baking tray (9" x 13") and bake for 25 minutes. In a skillet, cook ground beef, onions, and garlic. Drain excess fat. Stir in marinara sauce and pour the mixture over baked zucchini crust. Sprinkle with remaining cheese and top with chopped peppers. Bake 20 minutes more

Servings: 6
Each serving provides 1 Lean, 3 Greens, 3 Condiments and ⅙ Fueling

DESSERT

Salted Caramel Jicama Salad

Ingredients:
- 3 cups raw jicama, peeled and chopped (6 Greens)
- 1 1/2 cups 2% plain Fage Greek yogurt (1 Leaner)
- 1/2 tsp. vanilla extract (1/2 Condiment)
- 1/2 tsp. ground cinnamon (1 Condiment)
- 1 packet stevia (1 Condiment)
- 3 tbsp. caramel syrup, divided (1 1/2 Condiments)
- 1/2 tsp. coarse sea salt (2 Condiments)
- 28 toasted walnut halves (4 Snacks)

Directions:
In a medium bowl combine chopped jicama, yogurt, vanilla extract, cinnamon, stevia, 1 tbsp. caramel syrup and half of the chopped walnuts. Pour into a serving dish. Drizzle 2 tbsp. caramel syrup on top and then top with the other half of walnuts. Sprinkle sea salt on top.

Servings: 4
Each serving provides 1/4 Leaner, 1 1/2 Greens, 1 1/2 Condiments and 1 Fueling

Creamy Cheesecake

Ingredients:
- 1 cup 1% cottage cheese (2/3 Leanest Lean)
- 1 egg (1/3 Lean)
- 2 tsp. lemon juice (1 Condiment)
- 1 tsp. lemon zest (1/3 Condiment)

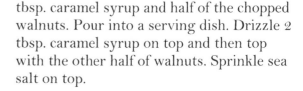

- 1 tsp. vanilla extract (1 Condiment)
- 3 packets Stevia (3 Condiments)
- 1/8 tsp. salt (1/2 Condiment)

Directions:
Preheat oven to 325. Blend all ingredients in a blender. Pour into two cocottes. Bake 50 minutes. Let cool completely.
Servings: 2

Servings 2
Each serving provides 1/2 Lean and 3 Condiments

Mousse au Chocolate

Ingredients:
- 1 packet of MF hot cocoa (1 Fueling)
- 1/2 cup pre-made sugar-free gelatin (cherry/strawberry) (1 Snack)
- 1 tbsp. light cream cheese (1 Condiment)
- 2 tbsp. to 1/4 cup cold water
- ¼ cup crushed ice (about)

Directions:
Mix it all in a blender.

Servings: 1
Each serving provides 1 Fueling, 1 Fueling, and 1 Condiment

Sweet Kugel

Ingredients:
- 6 cups spaghetti squash strands, cleaned and cooked (12 Greens)
- 8 packets stevia or sweetener of choice (8 Condiments)
- 1 tsp. cinnamon (2 Condiments)
- 1/4 tsp. nutmeg (1/2 Condiment)
- 1/8 tsp. salt (1/2 Condiment)
- 1 tsp. vanilla extract (1 Condiment)
- 1/4 cup reduced-fat cream cheese, softened (2 Healthy Fats)

- 2 whole eggs plus 4 egg whites (1 Leaner)
- 1 1/2 cups 2% cottage cheese (1 Leaner)

Directions:
Cooked Squash: Preheat oven to 375 degrees. Cut the squash in half and remove the seeds with a spoon. Place both halves, cut side down, in a baking pan, and bake for 50 minutes. Let it cool and scrape out the strands with a fork.
For the dessert: Blend smoothly sweetener, cinnamon, nutmeg, salt, vanilla extract, cream cheese, eggs, and cottage cheese. Stir the mixture with spaghetti squash and pour the mix into a casserole sprayed with cooking spray. Bake for 40 minutes.

Servings: 4
Each serving provides 1/2 Leaner, 3 Greens, 3 Condiments, and 1/2 Healthy Fat

Coconut Pie

Ingredients:
- 3 packets stevia (3 Condiments)
- 1 egg (1/3 Lean)
- 1 tbsp. melted light butter (1 Healthy Fat)
- 1 tsp. lemon juice (1/2 Condiment)
- 1/4 tsp. vanilla extract (1/4 Condiment)
- 1 cup cooked, shredded spaghetti squash (2 Greens)
- 1/4 tsp. coconut extract (1/4 Condiment)
- Dust of cinnamon

Directions:
Preheat oven to 350. Beat stevia and egg together, and then add lemon juice, vanilla, and butter. Beat until smooth. Pulse the spaghetti squash in a blender a few times. Stir in spaghetti squash. Pour the mixture into two cocottes. Dust the top with cinnamon and bake in preheated oven for 45 minutes

Servings: 2
Each serving provides 1/6 Lean, 1 Green, 2 Condiments, and 1/2 Healthy Fat.

Kabocha Yogurt Parfait

Ingredients:
- ½ cup kabocha squash cooked and mashed (1 Green)
- 2 tbsp. Maple Walnut Syrup (½ Condiment)
- ½ tsp. cinnamon (1 Condiment)
- 2 tbsp. unsweetened almond milk (⅛ Condiment)
- ½ cup low fat plain Greek yogurt (⅓ Leaner)
- ½ ounce chopped toasted walnuts (1 Fueling)

Directions:
Cooked Squash: Preheat oven to 375 degrees. Cut the squash in half and remove the seeds with a spoon. Place both halves, cut side down, in a baking pan and bake for 50 minutes. Let it cool and scrape out the strands with a fork.
Dessert assembly: Combine 1/2 cup squash, maple syrup, pumpkin spice, and milk. Layer half of the mix on the bottom of a glass. Then layer 1/4 cup of Greek yogurt. Then the other half of squash. Then 1/4 cup of Greek yogurt. Top with walnuts.

Servings: 1
Each serving provides 1/3 Leaner, 1 Green, 2 Condiments, and 1 Fueling

Pumpkin Pie

Ingredients:
- 2 cups roasted kabocha squash (4 Greens)
- 1/4 cup unsweetened cashew or almond milk (1/4 Condiment)
- 2 egg whites
- 1/2 tsp. ground cinnamon (1 Condiment)

- 1/2 tsp.. pumpkin pie spice (1 Condiment)
- 1/2 tsp. maple or vanilla extract (1/2 Condiment)
- 1 packet Stevia (1 Condiment)
- 28 Walnut halves (4 Snacks)

Directions:
Prepare kabocha:
Preheat oven to 375 degrees. Cut the squash in half and remove the seeds with a spoon. Place both halves, cut side down, in a baking pan, and bake for 50 minutes. Let it cool and cut off the skin with a knife. Measure out 2 cups of cooked squash, without the skin.
To make pies:
Preheat oven to 425 degrees. Spray 4 cocottes with non-stick cooking spray. Add the 2 cups of squash and the rest of the ingredients, except walnuts to the blender. Blend until smooth. Pour mixture into ramekins. Bake for 15 minutes. Then reduce heat to 350 degrees, remove ramekins from the oven and evenly distribute the walnuts on top of each ramekin. Bake for an additional 25 minutes.
Servings: 4
Each serving provides 1 Green, 1 Condiment and 1 Fueling

Cinnamon Jicama

Ingredients:
- 3 cups jicama peeled and cubed or sliced thin (6 Greens)
- 3 tbsp. melted light Butter with Canola Oil (3 Healthy Fats)
- 1/4 tsp. Apple-pie spice (1/2 Condiment)
- 1/4 tsp. ground cinnamon (1/2 Condiment)
- 3 packets stevia in the raw (3 Condiments)

Optional Toppings:
2 tbsp. caramel syrup (1 Condiment)

2 tbsp. Fat Free Whip (1 Condiment)

Directions:
Preheat oven to 350 degrees, and prepare a cookie sheet with parchment paper. Mix jicama, melted butter, cinnamon, apple-pie spice, and stevia in a bowl. Pour onto the cookie sheet. Bake for 20 minutes covered with foil. Uncover and bake for an additional 15 minutes.
Servings: 3
Each serving provides 2 Greens, 2 Condiments, and 1 Healthy Fat

Pumpkin Mousse

Preparation Time: 20 minutes
Cooking Time: 30 minutes
Servings: 4

Ingredients:
- 2 tsp. pumpkin pie spice
- 1 tsp. liquid stevia
- 2 cups heavy cream
- 15 oz. can pumpkin puree
- 15 oz. cream cheese
- 1 tsp. vanilla
- Pinch of Salt

Directions:
1) In a large bowl, blend pumpkin and cream cheese until smooth.
2) Add remaining ingredients and beat until fluffy.
3) Pipe it into the serving glasses and place in the refrigerator for 1 hour.
4) Serve and enjoy.

Nutrition: Calories 209; 1 serving healthy fat, 1 serving lean protein.

Mocha Mousse

Preparation Time: 20 minutes
Cooking Time: 30 minutes

Servings: 4

Ingredients:
- 1/2 cup coffee strong brewed (cooled)
- 2 cups heavy whipping cream
- 6 oz. unsweetened chocolate (chopped)
- 1 tsp. coffee extract

Directions:
1) In a large bowl, whip heavy cream and set aside.
2) Melt chocolate in a microwave-safe bowl.
3) Add coffee and coffee extract in melted chocolate and stir well.
4) Pour chocolate mixture into the whipped cream and stir until just combined.
5) Place in refrigerator for 30 minutes.

Nutrition: Calories 21; 2 servings healthy fat.

Chocolate Mousse 2

Preparation Time: 20 minutes
Cooking Time: 40 minutes
Servings: 4

Ingredients:
- 1/2 cup unsweetened cocoa powder
- 1 1/4 cup heavy cream
- 5 drop stevia
- 4 oz. cream cheese
- 1/2 tsp. vanilla

Directions:
Add all ingredients to the blender and blend until smooth.
Pipe mixture into the serving glasses and place them in the refrigerator for 1 hour.
Serve chilled and enjoy. Nutrition: Calories 254; 1 lean protein, 1 healthy fat.

SALTY

Prosciutto Wrapped Mozzarella Balls

Preparation Time: 10 minutes
Cooking Time: 10 minutes
Servings: 4

Ingredients:
- 8 Mozzarella balls (cherry size)
- 4 oz. bacon (sliced)
- ¼ teaspoon ground black pepper
- ¾ teaspoon dried rosemary
- 1 teaspoon butter

Directions:
1) Sprinkle the sliced bacon with ground black pepper and dried rosemary.
2) Wrap every Mozzarella ball in the sliced bacon and secure them with toothpicks.
3) Melt butter.
4) Brush wrapped Mozzarella balls with butter.
5) Line the baking tray with the parchment and arrange Mozzarella balls in it.
6) Bake the meal for 10 minutes at 365°F.

Nutrition: Calories: 323; 1 Green, 2 lean protein.

Garlic Chicken Balls

Preparation Time: 15 minutes
Cooking Time: 10 minutes
Servings: 4

Ingredients:
- 2 cups ground chicken
- 1 teaspoon minced garlic
- 1 teaspoon dried dill
- 1/3 carrot (grated)
- 1 egg (beaten)
- 1 tablespoon olive oil
- ¼ cup coconut flakes
- ½ teaspoon salt

Directions:
1) In the mixing bowl mix up together ground chicken, minced garlic, dried dill, carrot, egg, and salt.
2) Stir the chicken mixture with the help of the fingertips until homogenous.
3) Then make medium balls from the mixture.
4) Coat every chicken ball in coconut flakes.
5) Heat olive oil in the skillet.
6) Add chicken balls and cook them for 3 minutes from each side. The cooked chicken balls will have a golden-brown color.

Nutrition: Calories: 200; 2 lean protein, 2 healthy fat.

Garlic Chive Cauliflower Mash

Preparation Time: 20 minutes
Cooking Time: 18 minutes
Servings: 5

Ingredients:
- 4 cups cauliflower
- 1/3 cup vegetarian mayonnaise
- 1 garlic clove
- 1/2 teaspoon kosher salt
- 1 tablespoon water
- 1/8 teaspoon pepper
- 1/4 teaspoon lemon juice
- 1/2 teaspoon lemon zest
- 1 tablespoon Chives, minced

Directions:

1) In a bowl that is saved to microwave, add the cauliflower, mayo, garlic, water, and salt/pepper and mix until the cauliflower is well coated. Cook on high for 15-18 minutes, until the cauliflower is almost mushy.

2) Blend the mixture in a strong blender until completely smooth, adding a little more water if the mixture is too chunky. Season with the remaining ingredients and serve.

Nutrition: Calories: 178 2 Greens, 1 healthy fat.

Beet Greens with Pine Nuts Goat Cheese

Preparation Time: 25 minutes
Cooking Time: 15 minutes
Servings: 3
Ingredients:
- 4 cups beet tops, washed and chopped roughly
- 1 teaspoon EVOO
- 1 tablespoon no sugar added balsamic vinegar
- 2 oz. crumbled dry goat cheese
- 2 tablespoons Toasted pine nuts

Directions:
1) Warm the oil in a pan, and then cook the beet greens on medium-high heat until they release their moisture. Let it cook until almost tender. Flavor with salt and pepper and remove from heat.
2) Toss the greens in a mixture of balsamic vinegar and olive oil, then top with the nuts and cheese. Serve warm.

Nutrition: Calories: 215; 2 healthy fat.

Shrimp with Dipping Sauce

Preparation Time: 5 minutes

Cooking Time: 15 minutes
Servings: 6

Ingredients:
- 1 tablespoon reduced-sodium soy sauce
- 2 teaspoons Hot pepper sauce
- 1 teaspoon canola oil
- 1/4 teaspoon garlic powder
- 1/8 to 1/4 teaspoon cayenne pepper
- 1 lb. uncooked medium shrimp, peeled and deveined
- 2 tablespoons Chopped green onions
- Dipping Sauce:
- 3 tablespoons Reduced-sodium soy sauce
- 1 teaspoon rice vinegar
- 1 tablespoon orange juice
- 2 teaspoons Sesame oil
- 2 teaspoons Honey
- 1 garlic clove (minced)
- 1-1/2 teaspoons Minced fresh ginger root

Directions:
Heat the initial 5 ingredients in a big nonstick frying pan for 30 seconds, then mix continuously. Add onions and shrimp and stir fry for 4-5 minutes or until the shrimp turns pink. Mix the sauce and serve it with the shrimp.

Nutrition: Calories: 97; 4 healthy fat, 2 leanest protein, 1 Green.

Cheddar Drop Biscuits

Preparation Time: 30 minutes
Cooking Time: 15 minutes
Servings: 8

Ingredients:
- 1/4 cup coconut oil
- 4 eggs
- 2 teaspoon apple cider vinegar
- 1 1/2 cup coarse almond meal
- 1/2 teaspoon baking powder, gluten-free

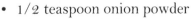

- 1/2 teaspoon onion powder
- 1/4 teaspoon salt
- 3/4 cup cheddar cheese
- 2 tablespoons Chopped jalapenos

Directions:
1) Line a sheet tray with parchment paper, and then preheat the oven to 400°F
2) Mix the wet ingredients in a bowl until combined, then reserve. Mix the dry ingredients in a separate bowl until combined, and then add them to the wet ingredients, stirring until incorporated. Fold in the cheddar cheese and jalapenos.
3) Drop the dough onto the parchment paper into eight roughly equal pieces, and then shape as desired once they are on the tray.
4) Bake until golden brown, 12-15 minutes. Rotate the tray halfway through baking so browning is even.

Nutrition: Calories: 260; 2 lean protein, 2 healthy fat.

Roasted Radish with Fresh Herbs

Preparation Time: 15 minutes
Cooking Time: 10 minutes
Servings: 4

Ingredients:
- 1 tablespoon coconut oil
- 2 oz. radishes
- 2 tablespoons Minced chives
- 1 tablespoon minced rosemary
- 1 tablespoon minced thyme

Directions:
1) Wash the radishes, and then remove the tops and stems. Cut them into quarters and reserve.
2) Add the oil to a cast iron pan, then heat to medium. Add the radishes, and then season with salt and pepper. Cook on medium heat for 6-8 minutes, until almost tender, then add the herbs and cook through.
3) The radishes can be served warm with meats or chilled with salads.

Nutrition: Calories; 123; 1 Green, 1 healthy fat.

ICY

Vanilla Avocado Popsicles

Preparation Time: 20 minutes
Cooking Time: 40 minutes
Servings: 4

Ingredients:
- 2 avocadoes
- 1 tsp. vanilla
- 1 cup almond milk

- 1 tsp. liquid stevia
- 1/2 cup unsweetened cocoa powder

Directions:
1) Add all ingredients into the blender and blend until smooth.
2) Pour blended mixture into the Popsicle molds and place in the freezer until set.
3) Serve and enjoy.

Nutrition: Calories 130; 2 lean protein, 2 healthy fat.

Chocolate Popsicle

Preparation Time: 20 minutes
Cooking Time: 40 minutes
Servings: 4

Ingredients:
- 4 oz. unsweetened chocolate, chopped
- 6 drops liquid stevia
- 1 1/2 cups heavy cream

Directions:
1) Add heavy cream into the microwave-safe bowl and microwave until it begins the boiling.
2) Add chocolate into the heavy cream and set aside for 5 minutes.
3) Add liquid stevia into the heavy cream mixture and stir until chocolate is melted.
4) Pour mixture into the Popsicle molds and place in freezer for 4 hours or until set.

Nutrition: Calories 198; 2 healthy fat.

Raspberry Ice Cream

Preparation Time: 20 minutes
Cooking Time: 30 minutes
Servings: 4

Ingredients:
- 1 cup frozen raspberries
- 1/2 cup heavy cream
- 1/8 tsp. stevia powder

Directions:
Add all ingredients into the blender and blend until smooth.

Nutrition: Calories 144; 1 healthy fat.

Chocolate Frosty

Preparation Time: 20 minutes
Cooking Time: 30 minutes
Servings: 4

Ingredients:
- 2 tbsp. unsweetened cocoa powder
- 1 cup heavy whipping cream
- 1 tbsp. almond butter
- 5 drops liquid stevia
- 1 tsp. vanilla

Directions:
1) Add cream into the medium bowl and beat using the hand mixer for 5 minutes.
2) Add remaining ingredients and blend until thick cream form.
3) Pour in serving bowls and place them in the freezer for 30 minutes.
4) Serve and enjoy.

Nutrition: Calories 137; 2 healthy fat.

SHAKES AND SMOOTHIES

Chocolate Cheesecake Shake

Ingredients:
- 1 packet Dutch Chocolate Shake (1 Meal)
- 1/2 cup 1% cottage cheese (1/3 Lean)
- 1/2 cup unsweetened almond milk (1/2 Condiment)
- 1/2 tsp. vanilla extract (1/2 Condiment)
- 1 cup ice

Directions:
Blend all the ingredients until smooth.

Servings: 1
Each serving provides 1, 1/3 Lean, 2 Condiments and 1 Snack

Fudge Balls

Ingredients
- 1 Chocolate Shake, divided (1 Fueling)
- 1 Chocolate Pudding (1 Fueling)
- 1 tbsp. chocolate syrup (1/2 condiment)
- 1 tbsp. Powdered peanut butter (1/2 snack)
- Little less than 1/2 cup water

Directions:
Reserve 2 tbsp. chocolate shake mix and set it aside. Combine the remaining chocolate shake mix, pudding mix, caramel or chocolate syrup, and Peanut butter powder in a small bowl. Add a little less than 1/2 cup of water little by little to have a very thick consistency. Form balls and roll them in the set aside mix. Refrigerate for 30 minutes.

Servings: 1

Each serving provides 1 Fueling, 1/4 Condiment and 1/4 Snack

Green Tea Smoothie

Ingredients:
- 1 Vanilla Shake (1 Fueling)
- 1/2 cup plain 2% Greek yogurt (1/3 Leaner)
- 1 cup unsweetened almond milk (1 Condiment)
- 1/2 tsp. Matcha Green Tea Powder (1/2 Condiment)
- 1 cup Baby Spinach (1 Green)
- Few cubes of ice

Directions:
Blend all the ingredients until smooth.

Servings: 1
Each serving provides 1 Fueling, 1/3 Leaner, 1 Green, and 1 1/2 Condiments

Pina Colada Shake

Ingredients:
- 1 Vanilla Shake (1 Fueling)
- 1/4 cup plus 2 tbsp. water
- 3 -4 ice cubes
- 1/2 cup diet ginger ale
- 1/4 tsp. pineapple extract (1/4 Condiment)
- 1/8 tsp. coconut extract (1/8 Condiment)
- 1/8 tsp. rum extract (1/8 Condiment)

Directions:
Blend all the ingredients until smooth.

Servings: 1

Each serving provides 1 Fueling and 1/2 Condiment

Pistachio Shake

Ingredients:
- 1 Vanilla Shake (1 Fueling)
- 1 1/2 tsp. Sugar-free pistachio pudding (1 1/2 Condiments)
- 1 cup baby spinach (1 Green)
- 1/2 cup unsweetened almond milk (1/2 Condiment)
- 1/2 cup water
- ice

Directions:
Blend all the ingredients until smooth.

Servings: 1
Each serving provides 1 Fueling, 1 Green, and 2 Condiments

Pumpkin Spice Frappuccino

Ingredients:
- 3/4 cups cold coffee
- 1/2 cup unsweetened cashew milk (1/2 Condiment)
- 1 tbsp. pumpkin puree (1 Condiment)
- 1/4 tsp. ground cinnamon (1/2 Condiment)
- 1/4 tsp. pumpkin spice (1/2 Condiment)
- 1 tbsp. Walnut Maple Syrup (1/2 Condiment)
- 1 pkg. Vanilla Shake (1 fueling)

Directions:
Blend all the ingredients until smooth.

Servings: 1
Each serving provides 1 Fueling and 3 Condiments

Root Beer Float

Ingredients:
- 1 Vanilla Shake (1 Fueling)
- 1/2 cup to 1 cup ice
- 1 cup diet root beer (make sure there are 0 carbs)

Directions:
Combine all the ingredients until smooth.

Servings: 1
Each serving provides 1 Fueling

Smooth Peanut Butter Cream

Preparation Time: 20 minutes
Cooking Time: 30 minutes
Servings: 4
Ingredients:
- 1/4 cup peanut butter
- 4 overripe bananas (chopped)
- 1/3 cup cocoa powder
- 1/4 tsp. vanilla extracts
- 1/8 tsp. Salt

Directions:
1) Add all ingredients into the blender and blend until smooth.
2) Serve immediately and enjoy.

Nutrition: Calories 101; 1 healthy fat, 1 Green.

Cantaloupe Kale Smoothie

Preparation Time: 5 minutes
Cooking Time: 5 minutes
Servings: 2

Ingredients:
- 8 oz. water
- 1 orange (peeled)
- 3 cups kale (chopped)
- 1 banana (peeled)

- 2 cups cantaloupe (chopped)
- 1 zucchini (chopped)

Directions:
Toss all your ingredients into your blender then process till smooth and creamy.
Serve immediately and enjoy.
Nutrition: Calories: 203; 2 Greens.

Mix Berry Cantaloupe Smoothie

Preparation Time: 5 minutes
Cooking Time: 5 minutes
Servings: 2

Ingredients:
- 1 cup alkaline water
- 2 fresh Seville orange juices
- ¼ cup fresh mint leaves
- 1 ½ cups mixed berries
- 2 cups cantaloupe

Directions :
1) Toss all your ingredients into your blender then process till smooth.
2) Serve immediately and enjoy.

Nutrition: Calories: 122; 1 Green.

Avocado Kale Smoothie

Preparation Time: 5 minutes
Cooking Time: 5 minutes
Servings: 3

Ingredients:
- 1 cup of water
- ½ Seville orange (peeled)
- 1 avocado
- 1 cucumber (peeled)
- 1 cup kale
- 1 cup of ice cubes

Directions:
Toss all your ingredients into your blender then process till smooth and creamy.

Nutrition: Calories: 160; 2 Greens, 1 healthy fat.

Apple Kale Cucumber Smoothie

Preparation Time: 5 minutes
Cooking Time: 5 minutes
Servings: 1

Ingredients:
- ¾ cup of water
- ½ green apple (diced)
- ¾ cup kale
- ½ cucumber

Directions:
1) Toss all your ingredients into your blender then process till smooth and creamy.
2) Serve immediately and enjoy.

Nutrition: Calories: 86; 2 Greens.

Refreshing Cucumber Smoothie

Preparation Time: 5 minutes
Cooking Time: 0 minutes
Servings: 2

Ingredients:
- 1 cup of ice cubes
- 20 drops liquid stevia
- 2 fresh lime (peeled and halved)
- 1 tsp. lime zest (grated)
- 1 cucumber (chopped)
- 1 avocado (pitted and peeled)
- 2 cups kale
- 1 tbsp. creamed coconut
- ¾ cup of coconut water

Directions:
1) Toss all your ingredients into your blender, then process till smooth and creamy.
2) Serve immediately and enjoy.

Nutrition: Calories: 313; 2 Greens.

Soursop Smoothie

Preparation Time: 5 minutes
Cooking Time: 0 Minutes
Servings: 2

Ingredients:
- 3 quartered frozen Burro Bananas
- 1-1/2 cups Homemade Coconut Milk
- 1/4 cup Walnuts
- 1 teaspoon Sea Moss Gel
- 1 teaspoon Ground Ginger
- 1 teaspoon Soursop Leaf Powder
- 1 handful Kale

Directions:
1) Prepare and put all ingredients in a blender or a food processor.
2) Blend it well until you reach a smooth consistency.
3) Serve and enjoy your Soursop Smoothie!

Nutrition: Calories: 213 2 Greens.

Cauliflower Veggie Smoothie

Preparation Time: 5 minutes
Cooking Time: 0 minutes
Servings: 4
Ingredients:
- 1 zucchini (peeled and chopped)
- 1 Seville orange (peeled)
- 1 apple (diced)
- 1 banana
- 1 cup kale
- ½ cup cauliflower

Directions:
1) Toss all your ingredients into your blender then process till smooth and creamy.
2) Serve immediately and enjoy.

Nutrition: Calories: 71; 2 Greens

Strawberry Milkshake

Preparation Time: 5 minutes
Cooking Time: 5 Minutes
Servings: 2

Ingredients:
- 2 cups of Homemade Hempseed Milk
- 1 cup of frozen Strawberries
- Agave Syrup to taste

Directions:
1) Prepare and put all ingredients in a blender or a food processor.
2) Blend it well until you reach a smooth consistency.
3) Serve and enjoy your Strawberry Milkshake!

Nutrition: Calories: 222; 1 leaner protein, 1 healthy fat, ½ Green.

Tiramisu Milkshake

Preparation Time: 5 minutes
Cooking Time: 0 Minutes
Servings: 2

Ingredients:
- 1 sachet Branded Frosty Coffee Soft Serve Treat
- ½ cup ice
- 6 ounces plain low-fat Greek yogurt
- ½ cup almond milk
- 2 tablespoons sugar-free chocolate
- 2 tablespoons whipped topping

Directions:
1) Place all ingredients except the whipped topping in a blender.
2) Pulse until smooth.
3) Pour in glass and top with whipped topping.

Nutrition Information: Calories: 239; 1 learner protein, 1 Green.

Cactus Smoothie

Preparation Time: 5 minutes
Cooking Time: 0 Minutes
Servings: 2

Ingredients:
- 1 medium Cactus
- 2 cups of Homemade Coconut Milk
- 2 frozen Baby Bananas
- 1/2 cup of Walnuts
- 1 Date
- 2 teaspoons of Hemp Seeds

Directions:
1) Take the Cactus, remove all pricks, wash it, and cut into medium pieces.
2) Put all the listed ingredients in a blender or a food processor.
3) Blend it well until you reach a smooth consistency.
4) Serve and enjoy your Cactus Smoothie!

Nutrition: Calories: 123; 2 Greens, 2 leaner protein.

Cucumber-Ginger Water

Preparation Time: 5 minutes
Cooking Time: 5 Minutes
Servings: 2

Ingredients:
- 1 sliced Cucumber
- 1 smashed thumb of Ginger Root
- 2 cups of Spring Water

Directions:
1) Prepare and put all ingredients in a jar with a lid.
2) Let the water infuse overnight. Store it in the refrigerator.
3) Serve and enjoy your Cucumber-Ginger Water throughout the day!

Nutrition: Calories: 117; 1 Green

SOFT BAKES

Banana Cheesecake Chocolate Cookies

Ingredients:
- 1 Brownie (1 Fueling)
- 1 Banana Pudding (1 Fueling)
- 2 tbsp. light cream cheese (2 Condiments)
- 5 tbsp. water

Directions:
Combine brownie mix with 2 tbsp. water. Spray a plate with Pam and spread the batter on to plate forming two circles. Microwave them on high for 1.5 minutes. In the meantime, combine pudding, cream cheese, and 3 tbsp. water to form a thick batter. Spread the batter evenly on cooled cookies.

Servings: 2
Each serving provides 1 Fueling and 1 Condiment

Pound Cake

Preparation Time: 20 minutes
Cooking Time: 70 minutes
Servings: 4

Ingredients:
- 4 eggs
- 1/4 cup cream cheese
- 1/4 cup butter
- 1 tsp. baking powder
- 1 tbsp. coconut flour
- 1 cup almond flour
- 1/2 cup sour cream
- 1 tsp. vanilla
- 1 cup monk fruit sweetener

Directions:
1) Preheat the oven to 350°F. Grease 9-inch cake pan and set aside.
2) In a large bowl, mix almond flour, baking powder, and coconut flour.
3) In a separate bowl, add cream cheese, butter, and microwave for 30 seconds. Stir well and microwave for 30 seconds more.
4) Stir in sour cream, vanilla, and sweetener. Stir well.
5) Pour cream cheese mixture into the almond flour mixture and stir until just combined.
6) Add eggs in batter one by one and stir until well combined.
7) Pour batter into the prepared cake pan and bake for 55 minutes.
8) Remove cake from the oven and let it cool completely.

Nutrition: Calories 211; 1 lean protein, 1 healthy fat.

Chocolate Cake with Peanut Butter Filling or Cream Cheese Icing

Ingredients:
- 1 Chocolate Chip Pancake (1 Fueling)
- 1 Brownie mix (1 Fueling)
- 1/4 cup plus 2 tbsp. water
- 2 tbsp. powdered peanut butter (1 Snack)
- 2 tbsp. Chocolate Syrup (1 Condiment)

Directions:
Mix the powdered peanut butter with 1 tbsp. water to get a thick paste. Combine pancake mix and brownie mix with 1/4 cup plus 2 tbsp. water. Place 1 full tbsp. of

batter in two separate muffin tins microwave friendly. Place half of the peanut butter in the centers of each container. Pour the residual batter to cover the peanut butter. Microwave for 2 minutes. Drizzle with 1 tbsp. chocolate syrup over each cake.

Servings: 2
Each serving provides 1 Fueling, 1/2 Snack with PB2, and 1/2 Condiment

Chocolate Chip Cakes

Ingredients:
- 1 packet Branded Brownie (1 Fueling)
- 1 packet Chocolate Chip Pancakes (1 Fueling)
- 1/4 tsp. baking powder (1/2 condiment)
- 1/4 cup water

Directions:
Preheat oven to 350°F. Combine the fuelings with the baking powder and water and stir. Divide batter into two muffin tins and bake for 20 minutes.

Servings: 2
Each serving provides 1/4 Condiment and 1 Fueling

Chocolate Chip Cookies

Ingredients:
- 1 Brownie Soft Bake (1 Fueling)
- 1 Chocolate Chip Soft Bake (1 Fueling)
- 4 tbsp. water

Directions:
Preheat oven to 375°F. Mix all the ingredients in a bowl and pour the mixture on a baking tray with parchment paper, forming 2 round cookies. Wet your hands because the batter is very sticky
Bake for about 14 to 15 min or until done.

Servings: 2
Each serving provides 1 Fueling

Chocolate Crunch Cookies

Ingredients:
- 1 Brownie Mix (1 Fueling)
- 1 crunch bar of your choice (1 Fueling)
- 3 tbsp. water

Directions:
Combine the brownie mix with water and set aside. Microwave the bar on a dish for 25 seconds. Add the melted bar to the brownie mixture and pour the mix on a plate with parchment paper creating 2 round cookies. spray. Microwave for 2 minutes.

Servings: 2
Each serving provides 1 Fueling

Chocolate Peanut Butter Cup

Ingredients:
- 1 package brownie mix (1 Fueling)
- 2 tablespoon powdered peanut butter (1 Fueling)

Directions:
Prepare a thick paste of peanut butter adding 1-2 tbsp. water to the powdered PB. In another bowl, combine the brownie mix with 3 tablespoons of water and spread half of the mix over the bottom of the silicone-baking cup. Spread the peanut butter paste over the chocolate mix bottom layer and cover with the residual cocoa mixture. Freeze for 1 hour.

Servings: 1
Each serving provides 2 Fueling

Brownie Pudding Cups

Ingredients:
- 1 Brownie Mix (1 Fueling)
- 1 Chocolate Pudding Mix (1 Fueling)
- 2 tbsp. caramel syrup (1 Condiment)

Directions:
Add 3 tbsp. water to the brownie mix.
Divide in two cocottes and microwave for 1 minute.
Prepare the chocolate pudding adding 1/2 cup of water to the mix and pour the pudding in the two cooled brownie cocottes.
Drizzle 1 tbsp. caramel syrup on top of each brownie pudding cups.

Servings: 2
Each serving provides 1 Fueling and 1/2 Condiment

Pudding Pies

Ingredients:
- 1 Packet Maple and Brown Sugar Oatmeal
- 1 Packet Banana Pudding (any flavor can be used)
- 1 Packet of stevia (1 condiment)
- 1/2 tsp. Baking Powder (1 condiment)

Directions:
Preheat oven to 350 °F.
Mix the entire ingredient except the banana pudding. Add 1/2 cup of water bit by bit until you get a sticky dough. Spray two cocottes with Pam and press the dough in them.
Bake for 10 minutes and let cool. In the meantime, prepare the banana pudding adding 4 oz. of water to the mix. Divide the pudding in the two cocottes and refrigerate 1 hour before serving.

Servings: 2

Each serving provides 1 Fueling and 1 Condiment

Peanut Butter and Cream Cheese Stuffed Brownies

Ingredients:
- 1 Brownie (1 Fueling)
- 1 tbsp. powdered PB (1/2 Snack)
- 1 tbsp. light cream cheese (1 Condiment)

Directions:
Follow the directions to make the batter of the brownie. Microwave the cream cheese for 10 sec to soften it and add the powdered PB to it. Add 1/2 tbsp. water if necessary.
Use the disposable containers given with the brownies sprayed with Pam and pour half the brownie mixture into it. Pour the peanut butter over it and cover with the residual brownie mix.
Microwave for 2 minutes.

Servings: 1
Each serving provides 1 Fueling, 1/2 Snack, and 1 Condiment

Peanut Butter Brownie Batter Greek Yogurt

Ingredients:
- 1 packet Brownie (1 Fueling)
- 5.3 oz. low fat plain Greek yogurt (1/2 Lean)
- 1 tbsp. powdered PB (1/2 Snack)

Directions:
Combine the ingredients in a bowl.

Servings: 1
Each serving provides 1 Fueling, 1/2 Leaner Protein, and 1/2 Snack

Sinful Brownie

Ingredients:
- 1 Brownie package (1 Fueling)
- 1 chocolate chip soft bake package (1 Fueling)
- 1/4 cup 1% cottage cheese (1/6 Leanest Lean)
- 1 tbsp. sugar-free caramel syrup (1/2 a Condiment)

Directions:
Prepare the brownie batter according to the directions and split it into two cocottes.
Prepare the soft bake batter according to the directions and set aside.
Blend the cottage cheese and the syrup, and then pour the mix over the brownie mix and top with the soft bake batter.
Microwave 1 minute.

Servings: 2
Each serving provides 1 Fueling, 1/12 Lean, and 1/4 Condiment

Chocolate Peanut Butter Cups

Preparation Time: 20 minutes
Cooking Time: 30 minutes
Servings: 4

Ingredients:
- ¼ cup unsweetened almond milk
- ¼ cup plain low-fat Greek yogurt
- A pinch of salt
- 4 packets stevia
- ¼ cup Branded PB2 2
- ¼ cup + 1 tablespoon water
- 1 Pinch salt

Directions:
1) In a bowl, combine the almond milk, Greek yogurt, cocoa powder, salt, and stevia. Mix until well combined.

2) In another bowl, mix the remaining ingredients until well combined.
3) In 14 mini muffin liners, spray cooking spray and pour in the chocolate mixture. Top with peanut butter mixture. Repeat layers.
4) Place in the freezer and freeze for 2 hours.

Nutrition: Calories: 120; 1 leaner protein, 1 healthy fat.

Chocolate Almond Butter Brownie

Preparation Time: 20 minutes
Cooking Time: 50 minutes
Servings: 4

Ingredients:
- 1 cup bananas (overripe)
- 1/2 cup almond butter (melted)
- 1 scoop protein powder
- 2 tbsp. unsweetened cocoa powder

Directions:
1) Preheat the air fryer to 325° F. Grease air fryer baking pan and set aside.
2) Add all ingredients into the blender and blend until smooth.
3) Pour batter into the prepared pan and place in the air fryer basket and cook for 16 minutes.
4) Serve and enjoy.

Nutrition: Calories 82; 1 healthy fat, 1 lean protein.

Peanut Butter Fudge

Preparation Time: 20 minutes
Cooking Time: 50 minutes
Servings: 4

Ingredients:
- 1/4 cup almonds, toasted and chopped

- 12 oz. smooth peanut butter
- 15 drops liquid stevia
- 3 tbsp. coconut oil
- 4 tbsp. coconut cream
- 1 Pinch of Salt

Directions:
1) Line the baking tray with parchment paper.
2) Melt coconut oil in a saucepan over low heat. Add peanut butter, coconut cream, stevia, and salt in a saucepan. Stir well.
3) Pour fudge mixture into the prepared baking tray and sprinkle chopped almonds on top.
4) Place the tray in the refrigerator for 1 hour or until set.

Nutrition: Calories 131; 3 healthy fat, 1 Green.

Almond Butter Fudge

Preparation Time: 20 minutes
Cooking Time: 30 minutes
Servings: 4

Ingredients:
- 3/4 cup creamy almond butter

- 1 1/2 cups unsweetened chocolate chips

Directions:
Line 84-inch pan with parchment paper and set aside.
Add chocolate chips and almond butter into the double boiler and cook over medium heat until the chocolate-butter mixture is melted. Stir well.
Pour mixture into the prepared pan and place in the freezer until set.

Nutrition: Calories 197; 1 healthy fat.

Shake Cake

Preparation Time: 5 minutes
Cooking Time: 30 Minutes
Servings: 2
Ingredients:
- 1 shake packet
- ¼ teaspoon baking powder
- 2 tablespoons egg beaters
- 2 tablespoons water
- 1 tablespoon reduced-fat cream cheese
- ½ packet Splenda

Directions:
1) Preheat the oven to 350° F.
2) Mix all ingredients in a bowl.
3) Pour in a muffin cup and bake for 15 minutes.

Nutrition: Calories: 271; 2 of leanest protein 1 of healthy fat.

Pumpkin Chocolate Cheesecake

Preparation Time: 5 minutes
Cooking Time: 30 Minutes
Servings: 2

Ingredients:
- 2 sachets Branded Essential Decadent Double-Chocolate Brownie
- ½ tablespoon unsalted butter (melted)

- 2 tablespoons cold water
- Cooking spray
- 1 cup non-fat plain Greek yogurt
- 3 tablespoons light cream cheese (softened)
- 3 tablespoons pumpkin puree
- 2 packets stevia
- ½ teaspoon pumpkin pie spice
- ½ teaspoon salt
- Vanilla extract

Directions:
1) Preheat the oven to 350° F.
2) In a bowl, combine the Chocolate Brownies, butter, and water.

3) Divide the brownie mixture into two mini spring-form pans. Press the mixture in the bottom of the pan to create a crust.
4) Bake for 15 minutes.
5) Meanwhile, combine the remaining ingredients in a bowl and mix until smooth. Divide mixture evenly among the two spring-form pans.
6) Lower the temperature to 300° F. Bake for 40 minutes.

Nutrition: Calories: 298; 2 of leaner protein, 2 healthy fat.

CRUNCHERS

Cinnamon Blondies

Ingredients:
- 1 packet of MF Cinnamon Pretzels (1 Fueling)
- 1 tablespoon eggbeaters
- 1/4 teaspoon baking powder (1/2 Condiment)
- 1 tablespoon water
- 1/8 tsp. Cinnamon (1/4 Condiment)
- 1 packet Stevia (1 Condiment)

Directions:
Preheat oven to 350°F. Crunch the MF pretzels into small pieces and then grind them into a powder using a blender. Add baking powder, eggbeaters, cinnamon, water, and mix until you get a "ball"

Put the dough in a glass baking dish, sprayed with cooking spray, forming a square approx.. 1/2" think-
Bake for 15 minutes.

Servings: 1
Each serving provides 1 Fueling and 1.75 Condiment

Crispy Buffalo Chicken Bites

Ingredients:
- 8 oz.. raw boneless skinless chicken breast cut into cubes (1 Leaner Lean)
- 2 tbsp. Hot Sauce (1 Condiment)
- 1 Bag Branded Parmesan Cheese Puffs (1 Fueling)
- 2 tbsp. Reduced-Fat Grated Parmesan Cheese (1 Condiment)

Directions:
Preheat oven to 350°F. Finely crush the Parmesan puffs using a blender. Mix the Parmesan cheese with the Parmesan puffs crumbs and set aside. Cut Chicken Breast into approximately 1-inch cubes. Toss chicken cubes with 2 tbsp. of Hot Sauce. Coat the chicken cubes with the parmesan crumbs and place them on a baking tray with parchment paper. Bake for 30 minutes.
Servings: 1
Each serving provides 1 Leaner Lean, 2 Condiments, and 1 Fueling

Haystacks

Ingredients:
• 1 Branded Hot Cocoa or Brownie Mix (1 Fueling)
• 1 Branded Cinnamon Pretzel Sticks, crushed (1 Fueling)
• 3 tbsp. water
• 1 packet Stevia - optional (1 Condiment)

Directions:
Crush the pretzels. In a bowl form a paste, combining hot cocoa or brownie mix with 3 tbsp. of water. Add 1 tbsp. powdered peanut butter and Stevia. Add the crushed pretzels and stir. Drop the haystacks on parchment paper forming 6 piles. Freeze for 30 minutes.

Servings: 2
Each serving provides 1 Fueling, 1/2 Condiment

PANCAKES

Pancake Cinnamon Buns

Ingredients:
• 1 MF Pancake Mix (1 Fueling)
• 1 packet Stevia (1 Condiment)
• 1/8 tsp. Baking Powder (1/4 Condiment)
• 1/4 tsp. Cinnamon (1/2 Condiment)
• 2 tbsp. water
• 1/4 tsp. Vanilla Extract (1/4 Condiment)
• 5 Sprays cooking spray (1/2 Healthy Fat)

Directions:
Put all ingredients in a small bowl except cooking spray and mix. Spray a small microwavable bowl with cooking spray and spoon the batter into it. Dust the top with cinnamon. Microwave for 40 seconds.
Servings: 1

Each serving provides 1 Fueling, 2 Condiments, and 1/2 Healthy Fat

Pineapple Mango Pancakes

Ingredients:
• 1 Pineapple Mango Smoothie (1 Fueling)
• 2 tbsp. water
• 1 egg white
• 1/4 tsp. baking powder (1/2 Condiment)

Directions:
Combine all ingredients in a small bowl and pour it on a hot skillet sprayed with cooking spray. Flip it when bubbles appear.

Servings: 1

Each serving provides 1 Fueling and 1/2 of a Condiment

Chocolate Cake with Peanut Butter Filling

Ingredients:
- 1 Chocolate Chip Pancake (1 Fueling)
- 1 Brownie mix (1 Fueling)
- 1/4 cup plus 2 tbsp. water
- 2 tbsp. powdered peanut butter (1 Snack)
- 2 tbsp. Chocolate Syrup (1 Condiment)

Directions:
Mix 2 tbsp. powdered peanut butter with about 1 tbsp. water to get a thick paste. Combine pancake mix, brownie mix, 1/4 cup plus 2 tbsp. water. Place 1/4 of batter in two brownie containers. Place half of the peanut butter paste in the centers of each brownie container. Pour 1/4 of batter over each brownie container to cover the peanut butter.
Bake 350 degrees for 15 minutes or until done. Drizzle with 1 tbsp. chocolate syrup over it

Servings: 2
Each serving provides 1 Fueling, 1/2 Snack, and 1/2 Condiment

Chocolate Chip Cakes

Ingredients:
- 1 packet Branded Brownie (1 Fueling)
- 1 packet Chocolate Chip Pancakes (1 Fueling)
- 1/4 tsp. baking powder (1/2 condiment)
- 1/4 cup water

Directions:
Preheat oven to 350 degrees. Combine the brownie mix to the chocolate chips, the baking powder, and water and stir until

combined. Divide batter into two brownie trays and bake for 20 minutes or until done.
Servings: 2
Each serving provides has 1/4 Condiment and 1 Fueling

Chocolate Chip Coffee Cake Muffins

Ingredients:
- 1 packet MF Cappuccino (1 Fueling)
- 1 packet MF Chocolate Chip Pancakes (1 Fueling)
- 1 packet of Stevia (1 Condiment)
- 1 tbsp. Egg Beaters
- 1/4 tsp. baking powder (1/2 Condiment)
- 1/4 cup Water

Directions:
Mix all the ingredients together and pour into a 4-inch dish, sprayed with Pam. Microwave on high for 2 minutes.

Servings: 2
Each serving provides 1 Fueling and 1 Condiments

Cinnamon Roll with Cream Cheese Icing

Ingredients:
- 1 pancake mix (1 Fueling)
- 2 tbsp. water
- 1/8 tsp. cinnamon (1/4 Condiment)
- 1 tbsp. light cream cheese (1 Condiment)
- 1 packet Stevia (1 Condiment)

Directions:
Combine pancake mix, cinnamon, half packet of Stevia, and water. Pour into a small microwavable container. Microwave for less than 1 minute. In a bowl, combine cream cheese and the rest of the stevia. Spread on the pancake.

Servings: 1
Each serving provides 1 Fueling, 2.25 Condiments

Vanilla Ricotta Crème Crepes with Chocolate Sauce

Ingredients:
- Chocolate Chip Pancake (1 Fueling)
- 1/4 cup water
- 1/4 cup part-skim ricotta cheese (1/4 Lean)
- 1/2 packet Stevia (1/2 Condiment)
- 1/8 tsp. vanilla extract (1/8 Condiment)
- 1 tbsp. Chocolate Syrup (1/2 Condiment)

Directions:
Combine chocolate chip pancake mix with water. Pour the batter on a non-stick skillet on high heat, sprayed with cooking spray. Combine ricotta cheese, Stevia, and vanilla extract. Put mixture inside the crepe. Drizzle 1 tbsp. chocolate syrup on top.
Servings: 1
Each serving provides 1 Fueling with 1.12 Condiments and 1/4 Lean.

Chocolate Chip Crepes with Cream Cheese Filling

Ingredients:
- Chocolate Chip Pancake (1 Fueling)
- 1/4 cup water
- 1 tbsp. light cream cheese (1 Condiment)
- 1 tbsp. fruit spread (1 Condiment)

Directions:
Combine chocolate chip pancake mix with water. Pour the batter on a non-stick skillet on high heat, sprayed with cooking spray. Combine cream cheese and fruit spread. Microwave for 15 seconds and stir until completely mixed. Put mixture inside the crepe.
Servings: 1

Each serving provides 1 Fueling with 2 Condiments

Butterscotch Crepes with Caramel Sauce

Ingredients:
- Pancake Mix (1 Fueling)
- 1/4 cup water
- Vanilla Pudding (1 Fueling)
- 1/2 cup water
- 1 tbsp. powdered peanut butter (1/2 Snack)
- 1 tbsp. Caramel Syrup (1/2 Condiment)

Directions:
Combine pudding with 1/2 cup water and 1 tbsp. powdered peanut butter. Chill in the fridge for half an hour.
Combine pancake mix with water. Pour the batter on a non-stick skillet on high heat, sprayed with cooking spray.
Spread 3 tbsp. of pudding in the crepe and drizzle 1 tbsp. caramel syrup over the top.

Servings: 1
Each serving provides 2 Fuelings, 1/2 Condiment, and 1/2 Snack

Pancake Muffins

Ingredients:
- 1 Pancake mix (1 Fueling)
- 1/4 cup water

Directions:
Combine pancake mix with water. Pour the batter on a non-stick skillet on high heat, sprayed with cooking spray. You can also Microwave for 1 1/2 minutes on high on a microwave-friendly container or a mug.

Servings: 1
Each serving provides 1 Fueling

Shake Cake

Ingredients:
- 1 Shake packet (1 Fueling)
- 1/4 tsp. baking powder (1/2 Condiment)
- 2 tbsp. egg beaters or egg whites (2/3 Condiment)
- 2 tbsp. water

Directions:
Preheat oven to 350°F. Mix all the ingredients and pour the batter into two muffin cups. Bake for 15 minutes.

Servings: 1
Each serving provides 1 Fueling and almost 1 Condiment

Pumpkin Waffles

Ingredients:
- 1 Branded Chocolate Chip or Golden Pancake (1 Fueling)
- ¼ tsp. pumpkin pie spice (1/2 Condiment)
- 1 tbsp. 100% canned pumpkin (1 Condiment)
- 1/4 cup water
- 2 tbsp. Walden Farms pancake syrup (1/2 Condiment)

Directions:
Spray a waffle maker with cooking spray and preheat. Then, combine all ingredients in a bowl, except pancake syrup, and pour half of the batter in the waffle maker. Cook evenly, remove it from the waffle maker, and cook the other half. Top with 2 tbsp. of pancake syrup.

Servings: 1
Each serving provides 1 Fueling and 2 Condiments

Zucchini Bread

Ingredients:
- Any Pancake packet (1 Fueling)
- 1/4 c. shredded, drained zucchini (1/2 of 1 Green)
- 2 tbsp. egg beaters
- 1.5 oz. water
- 1 packet Stevia (1 Condiment)

Directions:
Mix together and bake at 350 degrees for 20 minutes

Servings: 1
Each serving provides 1 Fueling, 1/2 of 1 Green, and 1 Condiment

BARS

Chocolate Crunch Cookies

Ingredients:
- 1 Brownie Mix (1 Fueling)
- 1 Crunch bar of your choice (1 Fueling)
- 3 tbsp. water

Directions:
Combine brownie mix with 3 tbsp. water and set aside. Microwave the crunch bar for 20 seconds on high until it is slightly melted and combine it with the brownie mixture. Place the mixture into two separate ramekins. Microwave for 2 minutes. Let cool for 5 min.

Servings: 3
Each serving provides 1 Fueling

Peanut Butter Crunch Bars or Cups

Ingredients:
- 1 Branded Chocolate Pudding (1 Fueling)
- 3 Branded Peanut Butter Crunch Bars (3 Fuelings)

Directions:
Make pudding as per instructions, in a medium-sized bowl and set aside.
Microwave the crunch bar for 20 seconds on high until slightly melted. Pour melted crunch bars into prepared pudding and stir until combined.
Pour mixture onto a cookie sheet lined with parchment paper. Make a rectangular shape and freeze for at least 2 hours. Cut into 4 equal portions.

Servings: 4
Each serving provides 1 Fueling.

Peanut Butter Cream Sandwiches

Ingredients:
- 1 Brownie Mix (1 Fueling)
- 1 Peanut Butter Crunch (1 Fueling)
- 3 tbsp. water
- 2 tbsp. powdered peanut butter (1 Snack)
- 1 tbsp. water
- 2 tbsp. cool whip (2 Condiments)

Directions:
Microwave on high the brownie and the peanut butter crunch for 20 seconds. Add 3 tbsp. water and mix. Spray a microwave-friendly tray with cooking spray and scoop the mixture into 4 portions. Microwave on high for 2 minutes. Mix powdered peanut butter and water to form a thick paste. Pour the paste on 2 cookies and add 1 tbsp. of cool whip to the other 2. Place peanut butter cookie on top of the cookie with whip cream.

Servings: 2
Each serving provides 1 Fueling, 1 Condiment, and 1/2 Snack.

5&1 MEAL PLAN

WEEK 1

Monday
- Fueling 1: Chocolate Cheesecake Shake
- Fueling 2: Banana Cheesecake Chocolate Cookies
- Fueling 3: Chocolate Chip Crepes with Cream Cheese Filling
- Fueling 4: Roasted Radish with Fresh Herbs
- Fueling 5: Pancake Cinnamon Buns
- L&G Meal: Easy BBQ Meatballs

Tuesday
- Fueling 1: Fudge Balls
- Fueling 2: Pound Cake
- Fueling 3: Pancake Muffin
- Fueling 4: Zucchini Bread
- Fueling 5: Chocolate Cake with Peanut Butter Filling
- L&G Meal: Jambalaya

Wednesday
- Fueling 1: Green Tea Smoothie
- Fueling 2: Chocolate Cake with Peanut Butter Filling or Cream Cheese Icing
- Fueling 3: Butterscotch Crepes with Caramel Sauce
- Fueling 4: Crispy Buffalo Chicken Bites
- Fueling 5: Pineapple Mango Pancakes
- L&G Meal: Springs Chicken

Thursday
- Fueling 1: Pistachio Shake
- Fueling 2: Chocolate Chip Cakes
- Fueling 3: Shake Cake
- Fueling 4: Haystacks
- Fueling 5: Chocolate Chip Cakes
- L&G Meal: Carne Guisada

Friday
- Fueling 1: Pina Colada Shake
- Fueling 2: Chocolate Chip Cookies
- Fueling 3: Pumpkin Waffles
- Fueling 4: Prosciutto Wrapped Mozzarella Balls
- Fueling 5: Cinnamon Roll with Cream Cheese Icing
- L&G Meal: Savory Salmon with Cilantro

Saturday
- Fueling 1: Pumpkin Spice Frappuccino
- Fueling 2: Chocolate Crunch Cookies
- Fueling 3: Zucchini Bread
- Fueling 4: Garlic Chicken Balls
- Fueling 5: Chocolate Chip Coffee Cake Muffins
- L&G Meal: Marinara Shrimp Zoodles

Sunday
- Fueling 1: Root Beer Float
- Fueling 2: Chocolate Peanut Butter Cup
- Fueling 3: Crispy Buffalo Chicken Bites
- Fueling 4: Garlic Chive Cauliflower Mash
- Fueling 5: Vanilla Ricotta Crème Crepes with Chocolate Sauce
- L&G Meal: Cauliflower Pizza Crust

WEEK 2

Monday
- Fueling 1: Smooth Peanut Butter Cream
- Fueling 2: Brownie Pudding Cups
- Fueling 3: Haystacks
- Fueling 4: Beet Greens with Pine Nuts Goat Cheese
- Fueling 5: Peanut Butter Fudge
- L&G Meal: Buffalo Cauliflower Bites – Air Fryer

Tuesday
- Fueling 1: Mix Berry Cantaloupe Smoothie
- Fueling 2: Peanut Butter and
- Fueling 3: Cream Cheese Stuffed Brownies
- Fueling 4: Prosciutto Wrapped Mozzarella Balls
- Fueling 5: Shrimp with Dipping Sauce
- Shake Cake
- L&G Meal: Mexican Style Shredded Pork

Wednesday
- Fueling 1: Cantaloupe Kale Smoothie
- Fueling 2: Pudding Pies
- Fueling 3: Garlic Chicken Balls
- Fueling 4: Cheddar Drop Biscuits
- Fueling 5: Almond Butter Fudge
- L&G Meal: Almond Maple Chicken

Thursday
- Fueling 1: Apple Kale Cucumber Smoothie
- Fueling 2: Sinful Brownie
- Fueling 3: Beet Greens with Pine Nuts Goat Cheese
- Fueling 4: Crispy Buffalo Chicken Bites
- Fueling 5: Cinnamon Blondies
- L&G Meal: Garlic Tilapia

Friday
- Fueling 1: Avocado Kale Smoothie
- Fueling 2: Peanut Butter Brownie Batter Greek Yogurt
- Fueling 3: Garlic Chive Cauliflower Mash
- Fueling 4: Zucchini Bread
- Fueling 5: Pumpkin Chocolate Cheesecake
- L&G Meal: Beef Pad Thai

Saturday
- Fueling 1: Soursop Smoothie
- Fueling 2: Chocolate Peanut Butter Cups
- Fueling 3: Shrimp with Dipping Sauce
- Fueling 4: Haystacks
- Fueling 5: Crispy Buffalo Chicken Bites
- L&G Meal: Sweet Chili Shrimp

Sunday
- Fueling 1: Refreshing Cucumber Smoothie
- Fueling 2: Chocolate Almond Butter Brownie
- Fueling 3: Cheddar Drop Biscuits
- Fueling 4: Prosciutto Wrapped Mozzarella Balls
- Fueling 5: Haystacks
- L&G Meal: Chipotle Mac and Cheese Waffles

WEEK 3

Monday
- Fueling 1: Cauliflower Veggie Smoothie
- Fueling 2: Peanut Butter Fudge
- Fueling 3: Roasted Radish with Fresh Herbs
- Fueling 4: Haystacks
- Fueling 5: Banana Cheesecake Chocolate Cookies
- L&G Meal: Buffalo Chicken Bake

Tuesday
- Fueling 1: Strawberry Milkshake
- Fueling 2: Shake Cake
- Fueling 3: Zucchini Bread
- Fueling 4: Prosciutto Wrapped Mozzarella Balls
- Fueling 5: Pound Cake
- L&G Meal: Springs Chicken

Wednesday
- Fueling 1: Cactus Smoothie
- Fueling 2: Almond Butter Fudge
- Fueling 3: Crispy Buffalo Chicken Bites
- Fueling 4: Garlic Chicken Balls
- Fueling 5: Chocolate Cake with Peanut Butter Filling or Cream Cheese Icing

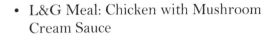

- L&G Meal: Chicken with Mushroom Cream Sauce

Thursday
- Fueling 1: Tiramisu Milkshake
- Fueling 2: Pumpkin Chocolate Cheesecake
- Fueling 3: Haystacks
- Fueling 4: Garlic Chive Cauliflower Mash
- Fueling 5: Chocolate Chip Cakes
- L&G Meal: Asian Beef Vegetable Skewers

Friday
- Fueling 1: Cucumber-Ginger Water
- Fueling 2: Cinnamon Blondies
- Fueling 3: Prosciutto Wrapped Mozzarella Balls
- Fueling 4: Beet Greens with Pine Nuts Goat Cheese
- Fueling 5: Chocolate Chip Cookies
- L&G Meal: Middle Eastern Salmon with Tomatoes and Cucumber

Saturday
- Fueling 1: Chocolate Cheesecake Shake
- Fueling 2: Crispy Buffalo Chicken Bites
- Fueling 3: Garlic Chicken Balls
- Fueling 4: Shrimp with Dipping Sauce
- Fueling 5: Chocolate Crunch Cookies
- L&G Meal: Thai Curry Shrimp

Sunday
- Fueling 1: Fudge Balls
- Fueling 2: Haystacks
- Fueling 3: Garlic Chive Cauliflower Mash
- Fueling 4: Cheddar Drop Biscuits
- Fueling 5: Chocolate Peanut Butter Cup
- L&G Meal: Cucumber Bowl with Spices and Greek Yogurt

WEEK 4

Monday
- Fueling 1: Green Tea Smoothie
- Fueling 2: Pancake Cinnamon Buns
- Fueling 3: Beet Greens with Pine Nuts Goat Cheese
- Fueling 4: Chocolate Chip Crepes with Cream Cheese Filling
- Fueling 5: Peanut Butter Fudge
- L&G Meal: Cabbage Wrapped Beef Pot Stickers

Tuesday
- Fueling 1: Pistachio Shake
- Fueling 2: Chocolate Cake with Peanut Butter Filling
- Fueling 3: Shrimp with Dipping Sauce
- Fueling 4: Pancake Muffins
- Fueling 5: Shake Cake
- L&G Meal: Almond Maple Chicken

Wednesday
- Fueling 1: Pina Colada Shake
- Fueling 2: Pineapple Mango Pancakes
- Fueling 3: Cheddar Drop Biscuits
- Fueling 4: Butterscotch Crepes with Caramel Sauce
- Fueling 5: Almond Butter Fudge
- L&G Meal: Chicken Teriyaki

Thursday
- Fueling 1: Pumpkin Spice Frappuccino
- Fueling 2: Chocolate Chip Cakes
- Fueling 3: Zucchini Bread
- Fueling 4: Shake Cake
- Fueling 5: Pumpkin Chocolate Cheesecake
- L&G Meal: Meatloaf

Friday
- Fueling 1: Root Beer Float
- Fueling 2: Cinnamon Roll with Cream Cheese Icing
- Fueling 3: Crispy Buffalo Chicken Bites

- Fueling 4: Pumpkin Waffles
- Fueling 5: Cinnamon Blondies
- L&G Meal: Salmon Florentine

Saturday
- Fueling 1: Smooth Peanut Butter Cream
- Fueling 2: Chocolate Chip Coffee Cake Muffins
- Fueling 3: Haystacks
- Fueling 4: Zucchini Bread
- Fueling 5: Crispy Buffalo Chicken Bites
- L&G Meal: Swiss & Tuna

Sunday
- Fueling 1: Mix Berry Cantaloupe Smoothie
- Fueling 2: Vanilla Ricotta Crème Crepes with Chocolate Sauce
- Fueling 3: Prosciutto Wrapped Mozzarella Balls
- Fueling 4: Haystacks
- Fueling 5: Crispy Buffalo Chicken Bites
- L&G Meal: Stuffed Bell Peppers with Quinoa

4&2&1 MEAL PLAN

WEEK 1

Monday
- Fueling 1: Chocolate Cheesecake Shake
- Fueling 2: Banana Cheesecake Chocolate Cookies
- Fueling 3: Chocolate Chip Crepes with Cream Cheese Filling
- Fueling 4: Roasted Radish with Fresh Herbs
- Fueling 5: Pancake Cinnamon Buns
- L&G Meal: Easy BBQ Meatballs

Tuesday
- Fueling 1: Fudge Balls
- Fueling 2: Pound Cake
- Fueling 3: Pancake Muffin
- Fueling 4: Zucchini Bread
- Fueling 5: Chocolate Cake with Peanut Butter Filling
- L&G Meal: Jambalaya

Wednesday
- Fueling 1: Green Tea Smoothie
- Fueling 2: Chocolate Cake with Peanut Butter Filling or Cream Cheese Icing
- Fueling 3: Butterscotch Crepes with Caramel Sauce
- Fueling 4: Crispy Buffalo Chicken Bites
- Fueling 5: Pineapple Mango Pancakes
- L&G Meal: Springs Chicken

Thursday
- Fueling 1: Pistachio Shake
- Fueling 2: Chocolate Chip Cakes
- Fueling 3: Shake Cake
- Fueling 4: Haystacks
- Fueling 5: Chocolate Chip Cakes
- L&G Meal: Carne Guisada

Friday
- Fueling 1: Pina Colada Shake
- Fueling 2: Chocolate Chip Cookies
- Fueling 3: Pumpkin Waffles
- Fueling 4: Prosciutto Wrapped Mozzarella Balls
- Fueling 5: Cinnamon Roll with Cream Cheese Icing
- L&G Meal: Savory Salmon with Cilantro

Saturday
- Fueling 1: Pumpkin Spice Frappuccino
- Fueling 2: Chocolate Crunch Cookies
- Fueling 3: Zucchini Bread
- Fueling 4: Garlic Chicken Balls
- Fueling 5: Chocolate Chip Coffee Cake Muffins
- L&G Meal: Marinara Shrimp Zoodles

Sunday
- Fueling 1: Root Beer Float
- Fueling 2: Chocolate Peanut Butter Cup
- Fueling 3: Crispy Buffalo Chicken Bites
- Fueling 4: Garlic Chive Cauliflower Mash
- Fueling 5: Vanilla Ricotta Crème Crepes with Chocolate Sauce
- L&G Meal: Cauliflower Pizza Crust

WEEK 2

Monday
- Fueling 1: Smooth Peanut Butter Cream
- Fueling 2: Brownie Pudding Cups
- Fueling 3: Haystacks
- Fueling 4: Beet Greens with Pine Nuts Goat Cheese
- Fueling 5: Peanut Butter Fudge
- L&G Meal: Buffalo Cauliflower Bites – Air Fryer

    124

Tuesday
- Fueling 1: Mix Berry Cantaloupe Smoothie
- Fueling 2: Peanut Butter and
- Fueling 3: Cream Cheese Stuffed Brownies
- Fueling 4: Prosciutto Wrapped Mozzarella Balls
- Fueling 5: Shrimp with Dipping Sauce
- Shake Cake
- L&G Meal: Mexican Style Shredded Pork

Wednesday
- Fueling 1: Cantaloupe Kale Smoothie
- Fueling 2: Pudding Pies
- Fueling 3: Garlic Chicken Balls
- Fueling 4: Cheddar Drop Biscuits
- Fueling 5: Almond Butter Fudge
- L&G Meal: Almond Maple Chicken

Thursday
- Fueling 1: Apple Kale Cucumber Smoothie
- Fueling 2: Sinful Brownie
- Fueling 3: Beet Greens with Pine Nuts Goat Cheese
- Fueling 4: Crispy Buffalo Chicken Bites
- Fueling 5: Cinnamon Blondies
- L&G Meal: Garlic Tilapia

Friday
- Fueling 1: Avocado Kale Smoothie
- Fueling 2: Peanut Butter Brownie Batter Greek Yogurt
- Fueling 3: Garlic Chive Cauliflower Mash
- Fueling 4: Zucchini Bread
- Fueling 5: Pumpkin Chocolate Cheesecake
- L&G Meal: Beef Pad Thai

Saturday
- Fueling 1: Soursop Smoothie
- Fueling 2: Chocolate Peanut Butter Cups
- Fueling 3: Shrimp with Dipping Sauce

- Fueling 4: Haystacks
- Fueling 5: Crispy Buffalo Chicken Bites
- L&G Meal: Sweet Chili Shrimp

Sunday
- Fueling 1: Refreshing Cucumber Smoothie
- Fueling 2: Chocolate Almond Butter Brownie
- Fueling 3: Cheddar Drop Biscuits
- Fueling 4: Prosciutto Wrapped Mozzarella Balls
- Fueling 5: Haystacks
- L&G Meal: Chipotle Mac and Cheese Waffles

WEEK 3

Monday
- Fueling 1: Cauliflower Veggie Smoothie
- Fueling 2: Peanut Butter Fudge
- Fueling 3: Roasted Radish with Fresh Herbs
- Fueling 4: Haystacks
- Fueling 5: Banana Cheesecake Chocolate Cookies
- L&G Meal: Buffalo Chicken Bake

Tuesday
- Fueling 1: Strawberry Milkshake
- Fueling 2: Shake Cake
- Fueling 3: Zucchini Bread
- Fueling 4: Prosciutto Wrapped Mozzarella Balls
- Fueling 5: Pound Cake
- L&G Meal: Springs Chicken

Wednesday
- Fueling 1: Cactus Smoothie
- Fueling 2: Almond Butter Fudge
- Fueling 3: Crispy Buffalo Chicken Bites
- Fueling 4: Garlic Chicken Balls
- Fueling 5: Chocolate Cake with Peanut Butter Filling or Cream Cheese Icing

- L&G Meal: Chicken with Mushroom Cream Sauce

Thursday
- Fueling 1: Tiramisu Milkshake
- Fueling 2: Pumpkin Chocolate Cheesecake
- Fueling 3: Haystacks
- Fueling 4: Garlic Chive Cauliflower Mash
- Fueling 5: Chocolate Chip Cakes
- L&G Meal: Asian Beef Vegetable Skewers

Friday
- Fueling 1: Cucumber-Ginger Water
- Fueling 2: Cinnamon Blondies
- Fueling 3: Prosciutto Wrapped Mozzarella Balls
- Fueling 4: Beet Greens with Pine Nuts Goat Cheese
- Fueling 5: Chocolate Chip Cookies
- L&G Meal: Middle Eastern Salmon with Tomatoes and Cucumber

Saturday
- Fueling 1: Chocolate Cheesecake Shake
- Fueling 2: Crispy Buffalo Chicken Bites
- Fueling 3: Garlic Chicken Balls
- Fueling 4: Shrimp with Dipping Sauce
- Fueling 5: Chocolate Crunch Cookies
- L&G Meal: Thai Curry Shrimp

Sunday
- Fueling 1: Fudge Balls
- Fueling 2: Haystacks
- Fueling 3: Garlic Chive Cauliflower Mash
- Fueling 4: Cheddar Drop Biscuits
- Fueling 5: Chocolate Peanut Butter Cup
- L&G Meal: Cucumber Bowl with Spices and Greek Yogurt

WEEK 4

Monday
- Fueling 1: Green Tea Smoothie
- Fueling 2: Pancake Cinnamon Buns
- Fueling 3: Beet Greens with Pine Nuts Goat Cheese
- Fueling 4: Chocolate Chip Crepes with Cream Cheese Filling
- Fueling 5: Peanut Butter Fudge
- L&G Meal: Cabbage Wrapped Beef Pot Stickers

Tuesday
- Fueling 1: Pistachio Shake
- Fueling 2: Chocolate Cake with Peanut Butter Filling
- Fueling 3: Shrimp with Dipping Sauce
- Fueling 4: Pancake Muffins
- Fueling 5: Shake Cake
- L&G Meal: Almond Maple Chicken

Wednesday
- Fueling 1: Pina Colada Shake
- Fueling 2: Pineapple Mango Pancakes
- Fueling 3: Cheddar Drop Biscuits
- Fueling 4: Butterscotch Crepes with Caramel Sauce
- Fueling 5: Almond Butter Fudge
- L&G Meal: Chicken Teriyaki

Thursday
- Fueling 1: Pumpkin Spice Frappuccino
- Fueling 2: Chocolate Chip Cakes
- Fueling 3: Zucchini Bread
- Fueling 4: Shake Cake
- Fueling 5: Pumpkin Chocolate Cheesecake
- L&G Meal: Meatloaf

Friday
- Fueling 1: Root Beer Float
- Fueling 2: Cinnamon Roll with Cream Cheese Icing
- Fueling 3: Crispy Buffalo Chicken Bites

- Fueling 4: Pumpkin Waffles
- Fueling 5: Cinnamon Blondies
- L&G Meal: Salmon Florentine

Saturday
- Fueling 1: Smooth Peanut Butter Cream
- Fueling 2: Chocolate Chip Coffee Cake Muffins
- Fueling 3: Haystacks
- Fueling 4: Zucchini Bread
- Fueling 5: Crispy Buffalo Chicken Bites
- L&G Meal: Swiss & Tuna

Sunday
- Fueling 1: Mix Berry Cantaloupe Smoothie
- Fueling 2: Vanilla Ricotta Crème Crepes with Chocolate Sauce
- Fueling 3: Prosciutto Wrapped Mozzarella Balls
- Fueling 4: Haystacks
- Fueling 5: Crispy Buffalo Chicken Bites
- L&G Meal: Stuffed Bell Peppers with Quinoa

CONCLUSION

The Lean and Green Diet is a series of three programs, two of which focus on losing weight and the other is perfect for weight management. To promote weight loss, the programs are high in protein and low in carbohydrates and calories. Each plan requires that you consume at least half of your food in the form of prepackaged foods. Since the menu calls for carbohydrates, proteins, and fats, it is therefore a reasonably healthy diet in terms of food group consumption.

At this moment of your journey, you must recognize that you've overcome the hardest task, i.e., the first dreadful step towards health and wellbeing. Please remember that this alone is a commendable feat and whoever survives the first step can survive the rest and come out at the other side thinner, stronger, wiser, happier, and overall better.

If you need motivation or if you doubt yourself before joining the amazing Community, rest assured that this is the right thing to do for your health and wellness. The coaches are always there for you to support you, guide you, and streamline your journey towards personal growth. Never be shy to reach out to them if you need any kind of help.

Remember, the journey of a thousand miles still begins with just a single step indeed. So, stand tall, be confident, and just go ahead each day with your ideal vision of yourself in your mind, moving a bit closer to your goals every day.

The program has earned worldwide acclaims for its ability to deliver sustainable results without complicating the meal program for people. It places very few restrictions on food and inspires people to choose a healthier version of their daily food without compromising on taste and nutrition.

The Lean and Green Diet program is a stress-free and easy to follow program. It is a cool way to start a journey to your lifelong transformation.

APPENDIX: SHOPPING LIST

Foods that you always need to be in your pantry

Meat

- Lamb tenderloin
- Roasted beef
- Pork chops
- Chicken breast
- Buffalo meat
- Turkey
- Deer
- Sword fish
- Salmon
- Tuna
- Trout
- Halibut
- Mackerel
- Crab
- Shrimp

Fruits/Veggies

- Spinach
- Cauliflower
- Onions
- Broccoli
- Cucumbers
- Radishes
- Mushrooms
- Tomatoes
- Rosemary
- Basil leaves
- Scallop
- Eggplant
- Zucchini
- Mint leaves
- Garlic
- Berries
- Avocado

- Rasp berries
- Straw berries
- Soursop
- Banana

Others

- Kale
- Greek yogurt
- Cheddar cheese
- Salt
- Cooking oil
- Cooking sprays
- Syrups
- Cumin
- Salsa
- Eggs
- Tofu
- Cactus
- Tempeh
- Sunflower seeds
- Paprika
- Chili powder
- Nuts (pine nuts)
- Ginger

Made in the USA
Coppell, TX
06 June 2022

78532226R00072